Starfish

K1

Student's Book

Catalogue Publication Data

Starfish K1 Student's Book
Author: Angela Llanas, Libby Williams
Pearson Educación de México, S.A. de C.V., 2019
ISBN: 978-607-32-4666-8
Area: ELT
Format: 30.5 x 23.5 cm Page count: 248

Managing Director: Sergio Fonseca ■ **Innovation & Learning Delivery Director:** Alan David Palau ■ **Regional Content Manager - English:** Andrew Starling ■ **Innovation and Implementation Manager:** Gonzalo Pastor ■ **Publisher:** Hened Manzur ■ **Content Development:** Canda Machado ■ **Content Support:** Silvia Barrientos ■ **Art and Design Coordinator:** Juan Manuel Santamaría ■ **Design Process Supervisor:** Salvador Pereira ■ **Layout:** Berenice Hinojosa ■ **Cover Design:** BrandB/Fenómeno ■ **Interior Design:** BrandB/Fenómeno ■ **Photo Research:** Salvador Pereira ■ **Photo Credits:** Shutterstock ■ **Illustrations:** Ana Elena García, Belén García, Carmen López, Gerardo Sánchez, Miguel Ángel Chávez, Herenia González, Jaqueline Velázquez, José de Santiago Torices, Marcela Gómez, Olivia González, Sheila Cabeza de Vaca, Tania Dinorah Recio, Víctor Sandoval, Ximena García Trigos

The Publisher wishes to acknowledge the valuable collaboration of **Sophie Angerman**, author of the Mathematics program.

First published, 2019

ISBN PRINT BOOK: 978-607-32-4666-8

Esta obra se terminó de imprimir en abril del 2022 en los talleres de:
Diversidad Gráfica S.A. de C.V.
Privada de Av. 11 #1, Col. El Vergel, Iztapalapa, C.P. 09880,
México, Ciudad de México, Tel. 5426-6386
www.diversidadgrafica.com

D.R. © 2019 por Pearson Educación de México, S.A. de C.V.
Avenida Antonio Dovalí Jaime #70
Torre B, Piso 6, Colonia Zedec Ed. Plaza Santa Fe
Delegación Álvaro Obregón, México, Ciudad de México, C. P. 01210

www.pearsonelt.com

Impreso en México. *Printed in Mexico.*

1 2 3 4 5 6 7 8 9 0 - 22 21 20 19

Pearson Hispanoamérica
Argentina ■ Belice ■ Bolivia ■ Chile ■ Colombia ■ Costa Rica ■ Cuba ■ República Dominicana ■ Ecuador ■ El Salvador ■ Guatemala ■ Honduras ■ México ■ Nicaragua ■ Panamá ■ Paraguay ■ Perú ■ Uruguay ■ Venezuela

Contents

Unit		Page
1	How are we all similar?	4
2	How are we all different?	29
3	What is a family?	54
4	Do you share your toys? Why?	79
5	How do you help at home?	116
6	How do you take care of your pet?	141
7	What is your favorite food?	178
8	What do you like about school?	203

Unit 1 How are we all similar?

Look, listen, and say. 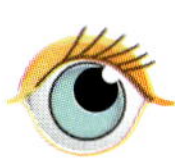 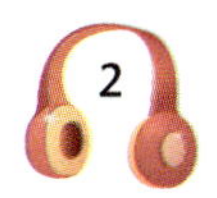 

Color the apples.

Objectives: Understand a story.

Listen. Follow the ants and color.

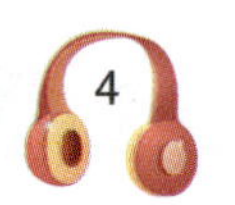

What color is your apple?

Objectives: Learn words with short /a/ sound.

Point, say, and color the pattern.  

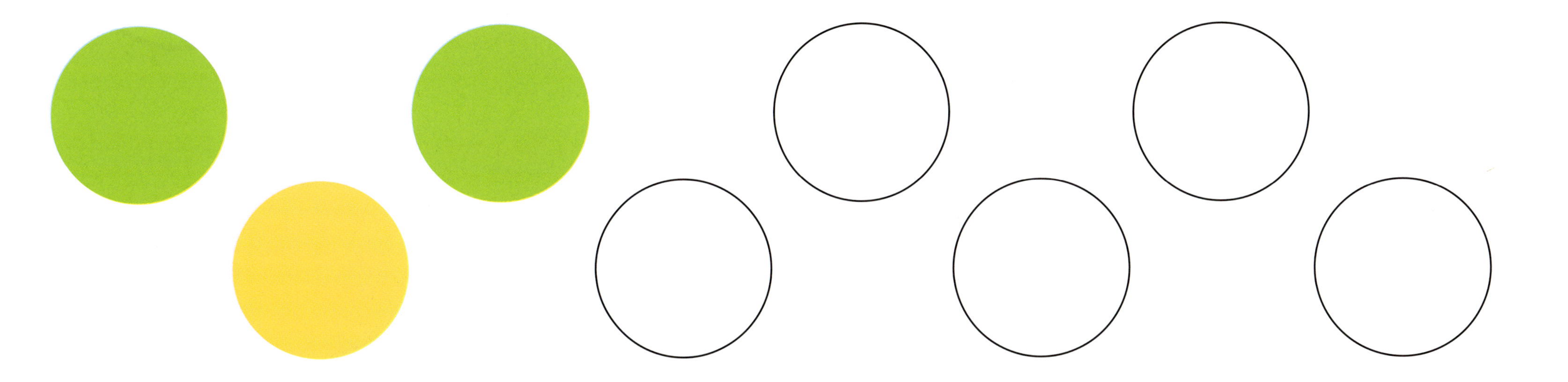

Objectives: Follow and color a simple pattern.

Listen, point, and say.  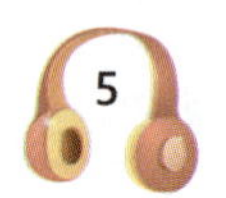

Color. 

Hello

Good-bye

Think!
Do animals say hello? How?

Objectives: Greet and say good-bye.

What's missing? Complete the pictures. 

Exploration and Knowing of the World

Learning to Do

Think!
What do our faces have in common?

Objectives: Identify different faces.

Listen and repeat. Circle the correct word.

Please.

Thank you.

Please.

Thank you.

Think!
When do you say *please* and *thank you*?

Act out the conversation.

Objectives: Use polite conventions.

Listen, point, and say. Color.

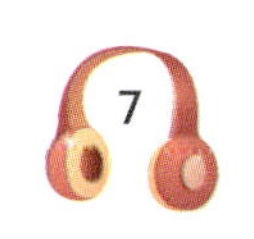

Draw another ant.

Objectives: Understand a story.

Color the cat. Trace. Listen and say.

Objectives: Short /a/ sound.

Color the squares green.
Color the circles blue.

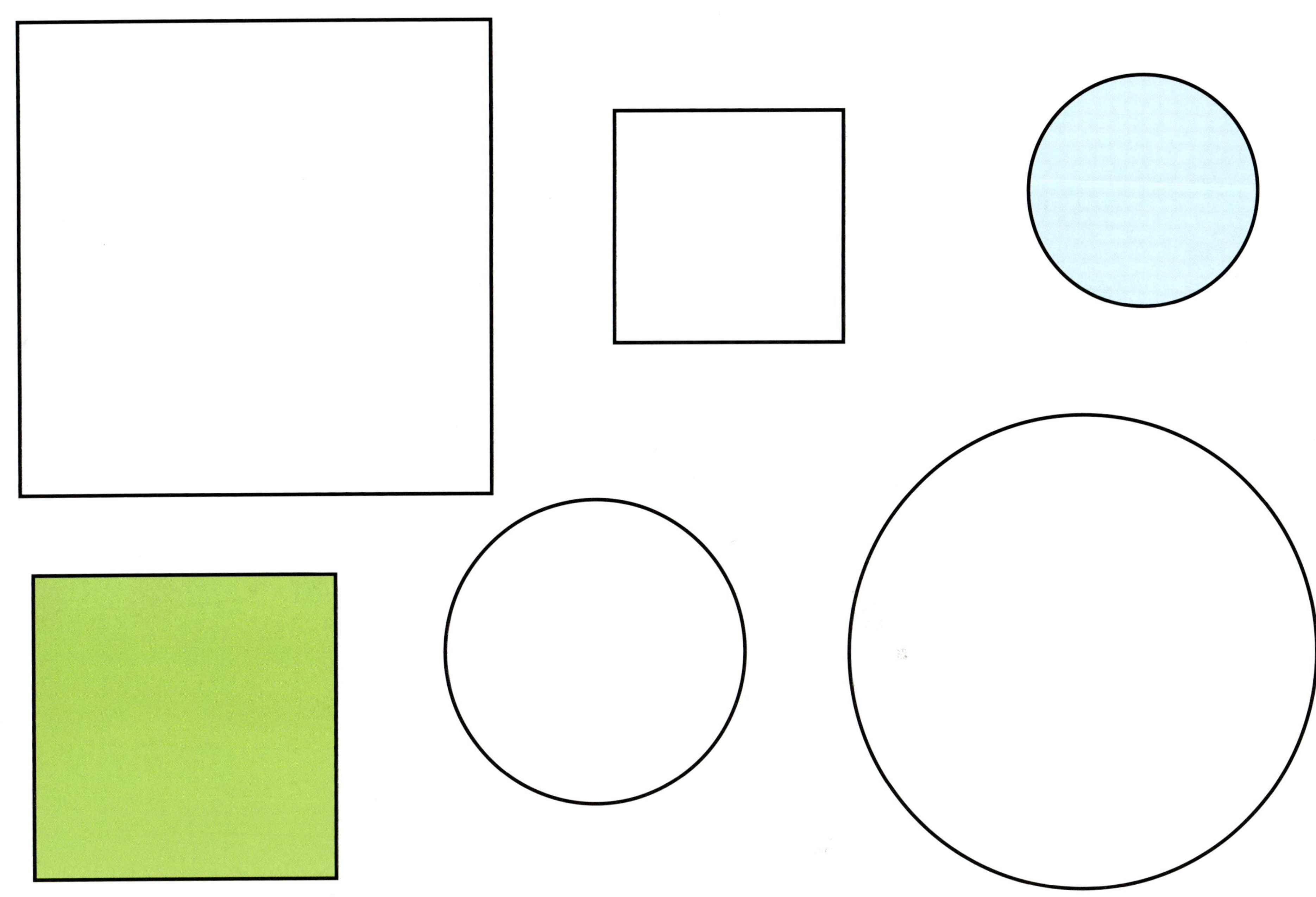

Objectives: Identify and name circles and squares.

Listen and point.  

Write your name. 

Objectives: Say their names.

Find the different pictures and circle.

Exploration and Knowing of the World

Learning to Do

Think!
How are people's and animal's faces different?

Objectives: Identify different faces.

Color each crayon a different color.
Play the game.

Think!
What games do you like to play?

Objectives: Play a game.

Listen. Circle what's wrong. 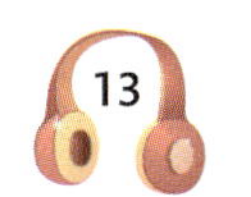 

Literacy

Learning to Know

Act out the story. 

Objectives: Understand a story.

Circle the *a*'s. Listen and say.  

bat

cat

hat

apple

ant

Objectives: Identify and say words with short /a/ sound.

Trace, color, and match.   

2

1

3

Objectives: Match sets of objects to the corresponding number.

Talk about the pictures. 

Draw yourself. Talk about your picture. 

Objectives: Say if they are boys or girls.

Talk about the faces. Match the parts of the face.

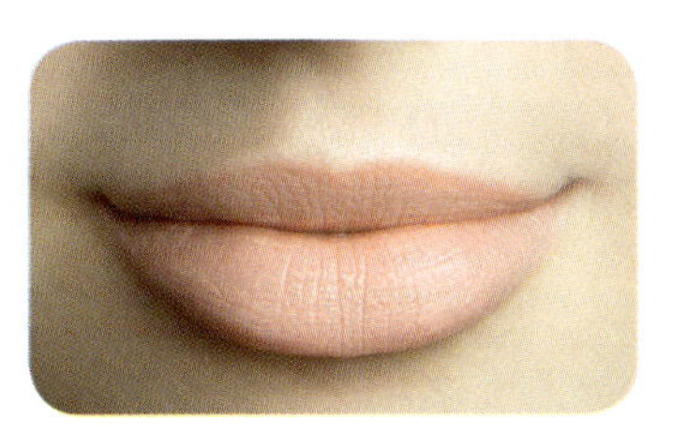

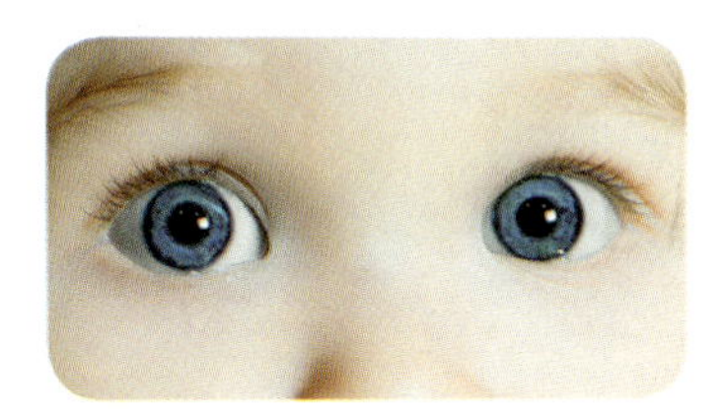

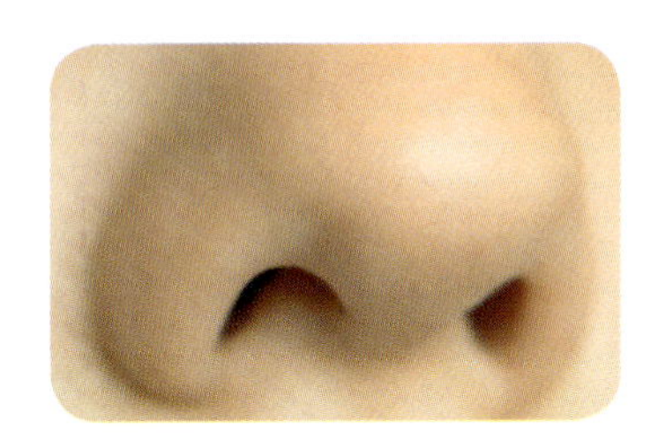

What's different?

Think!
What animals have two eyes, a nose, and a mouth?

Objectives: Identify different faces.

Talk about the pictures. Match.

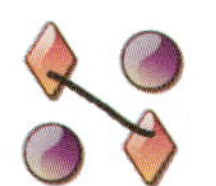

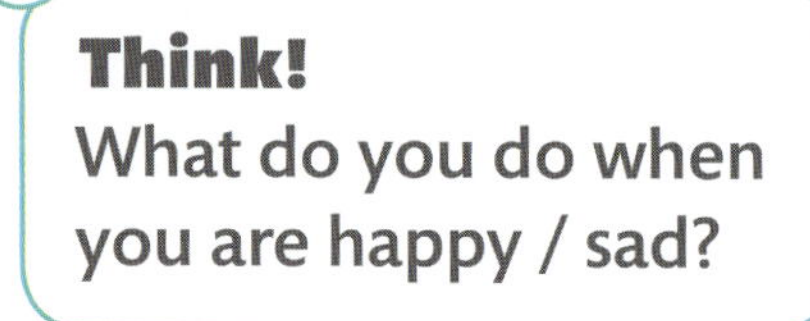

Think!
What do you do when you are happy / sad?

Objectives: Express emotions.

Listen. Tell the story. Color using finger paint.

Phonemic Awareness

Learning to Know

Draw a picture of a word with an /a/ sound. Tell a friend.

Objectives: Short /a/ sound.

Point. Say the school objects. Cut and paste.

Listen, point, and say.  

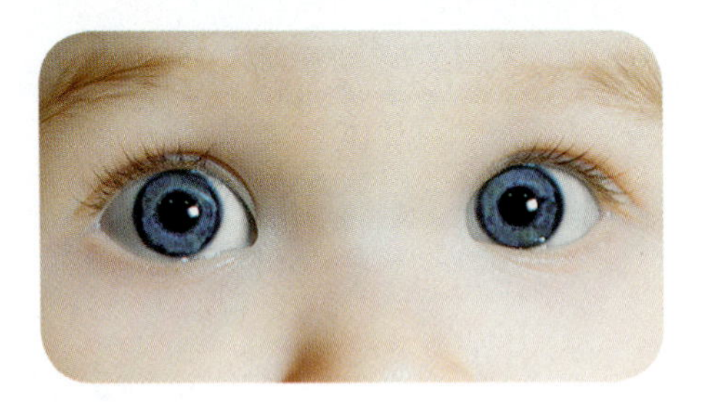
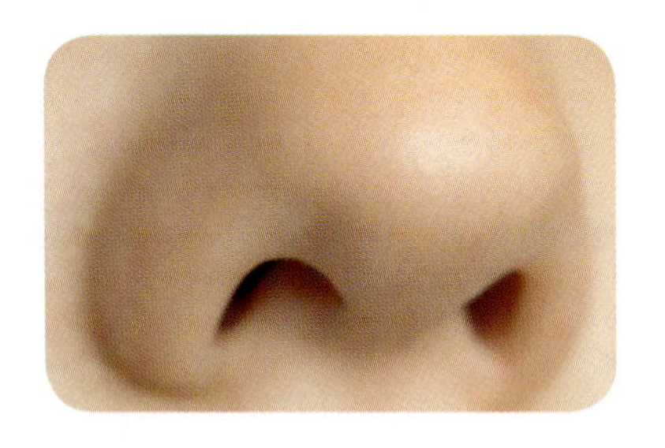
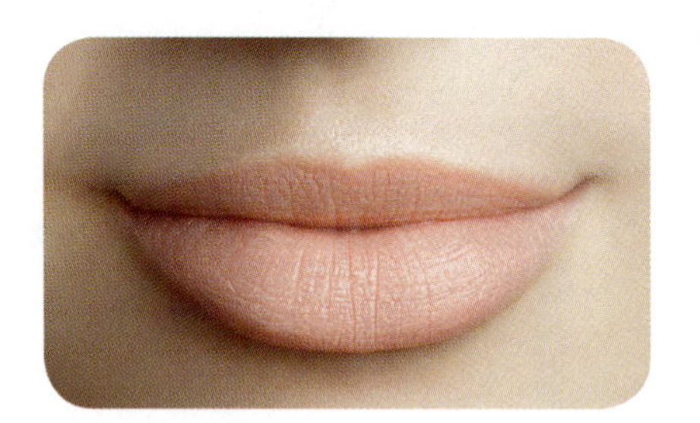

Language Instruction and Communication

Learning to Know

Match and say.  

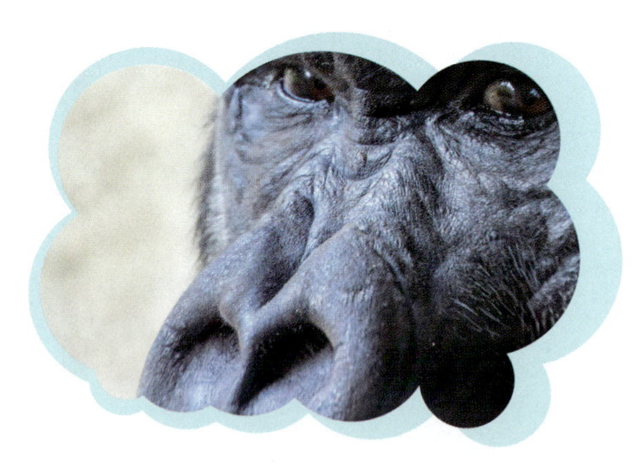

Objectives: Parts of the face.

Talk about faces from the past and the present.

Exploration and Knowing of the World

Learning to Do

Think!
How are faces from the past similar to our faces?

Circle the faces from the past.

Objectives: Identify different faces.

Talk about the pictures. Circle the things that you share with your friends.

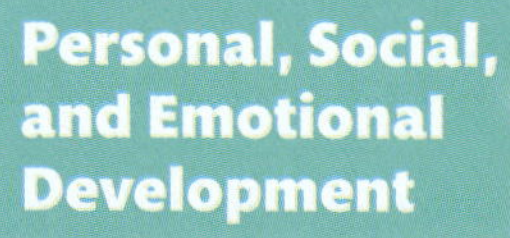

Personal, Social, and Emotional Development

Learning to Live Together
Learning to Live with Others

Think!
How do you feel when you share your things?

Objectives: Recognize that we all have feelings.

Unit 2 How are we all different?

Look and listen. 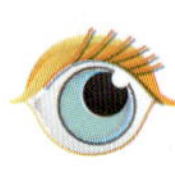 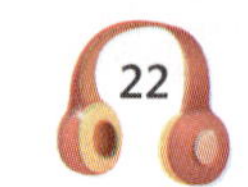

The elephant's name is Ellie.

Think!
How do the girl and mother feel?

Sing the song. 

Objectives: Understand a story.

Draw an elephant. Color.  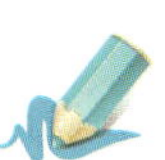

elephant

Think!
What name will you give your elephant?

Complete the word. 

Objectives: Short /e/ sound.

Count, match, and color. 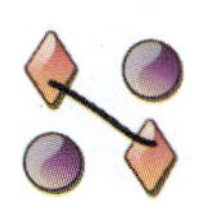 

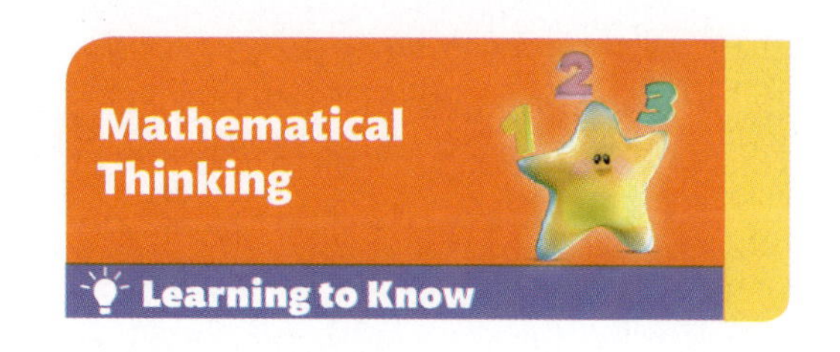

1

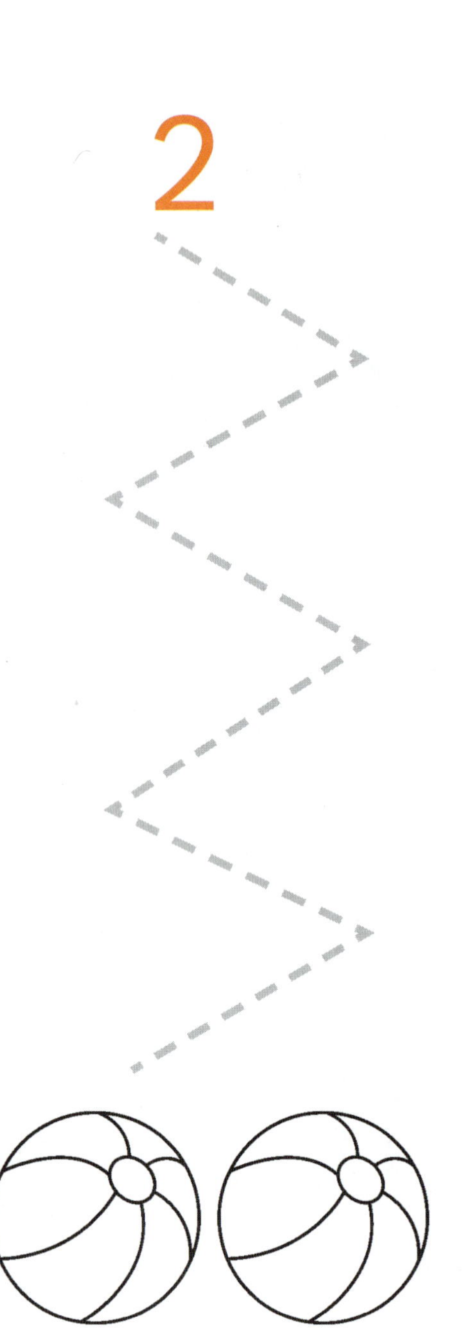

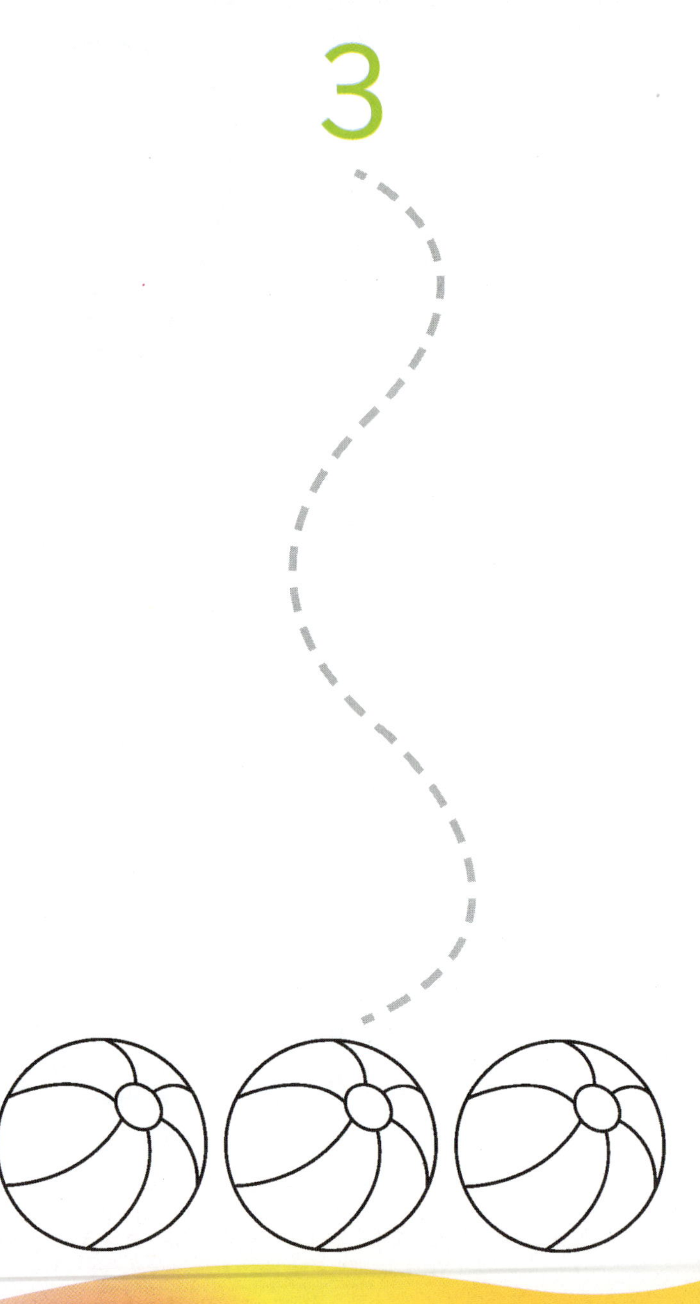

Objectives: Match objects and numbers.

Circle what the girl is saying. 

hello
bye

hello
bye

Objectives: Greet and say good-bye.

Match the parts of the head.

Exploration and Knowing of the World

Learning to Do

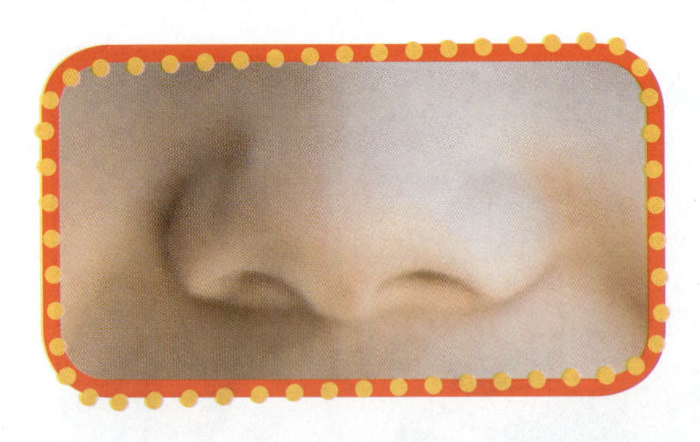

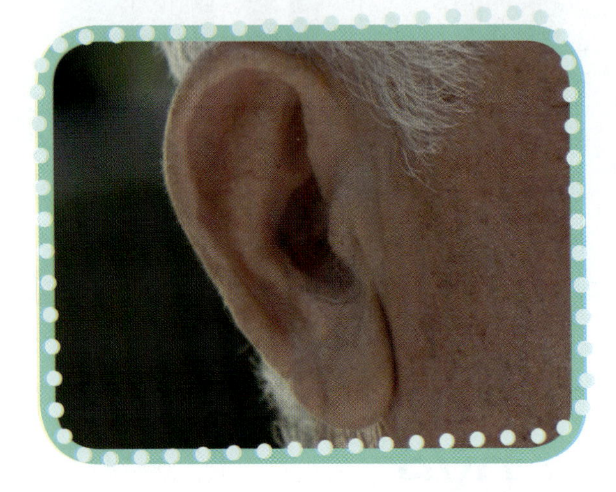

Think!
How are their faces different?

Objectives: Identify parts of the head.

Match the boy's front to his back. 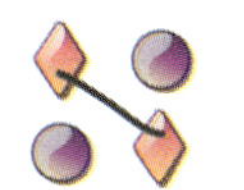

Personal, Social, and Emotional Development 

Learning to Live Together
Learning to Live with Others

Draw your face. Listen.  

Objectives: Recognize oneself in the mirror.

Look and listen. What are the children eating? Color.

Listen and sing.

Objectives: Understand a story.

● Color the big eggs green and the little eggs orange. Trace the e.

Think!
Do you like eggs?

Look and extend the pattern.

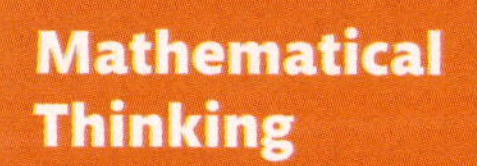

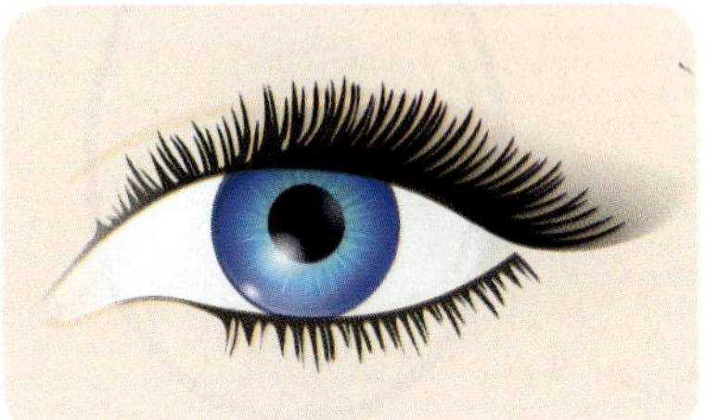

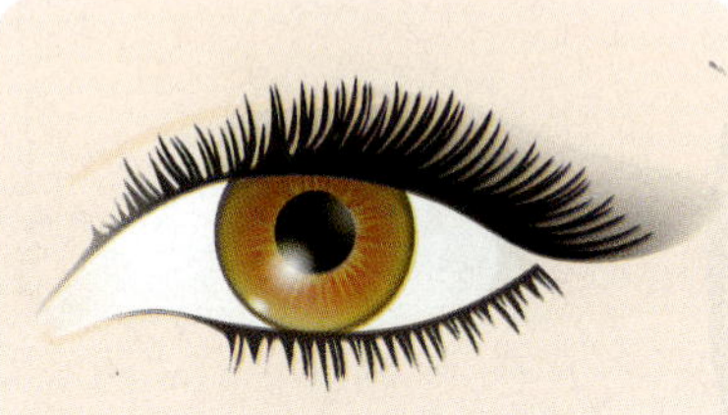

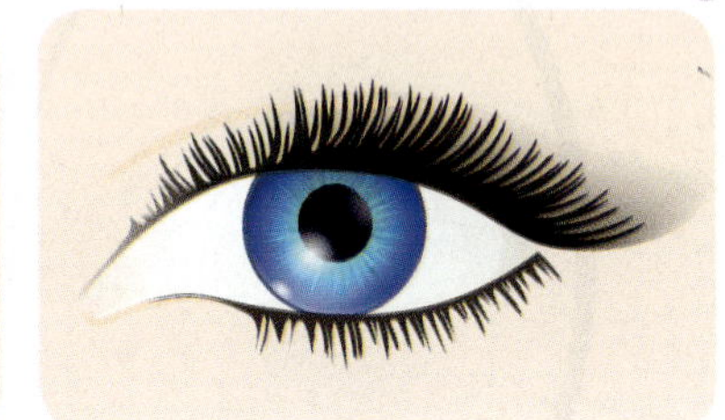

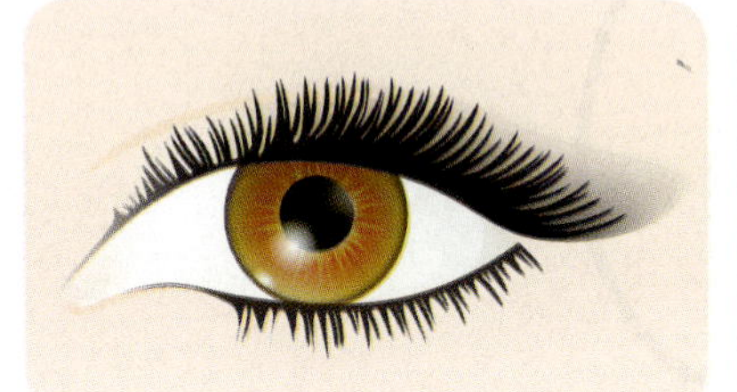

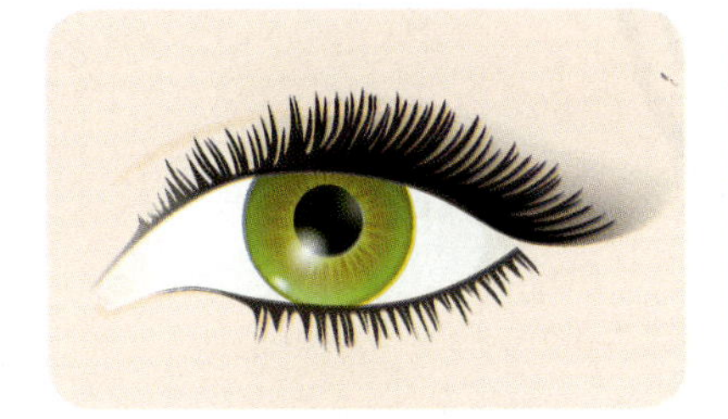

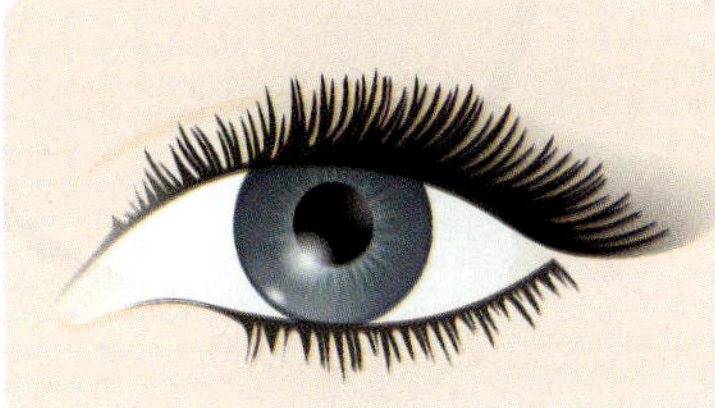

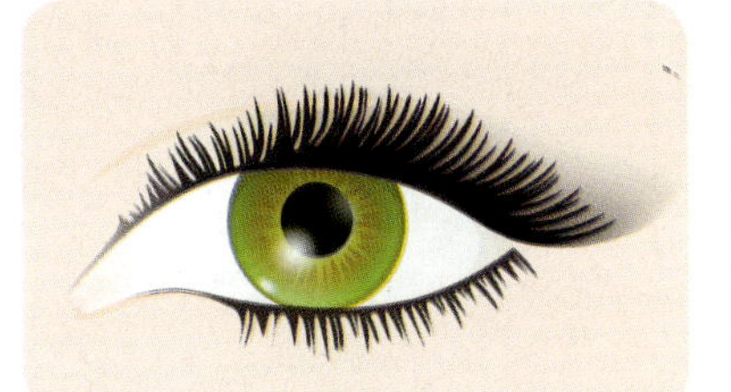

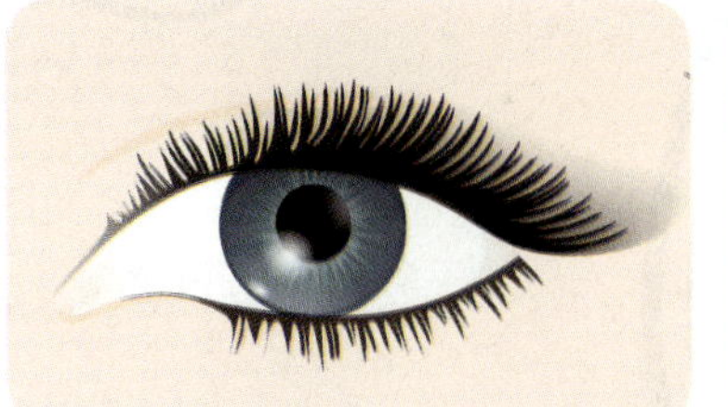

Objectives: Extend a simple pattern.

- Circle the girl and draw a triangle around the boy.

- Match the names to the pictures. 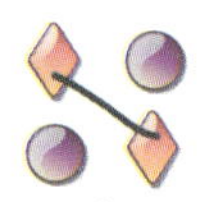

Think!
Are you a boy or a girl?
Is your best friend a boy or a girl?

Objectives: Say their names. Say if they are boys or girls (am, is, are).

Complete the person. Listen. Do the actions. 31

Think!
How many arms and legs do you have?

Circle the fingers and toes.

Objectives: Identify parts of the body.

Listen to your teacher. Play the game.

Objectives: Play games. Follow rules and directions.

Listen and circle the correct pictures. Tell the story.

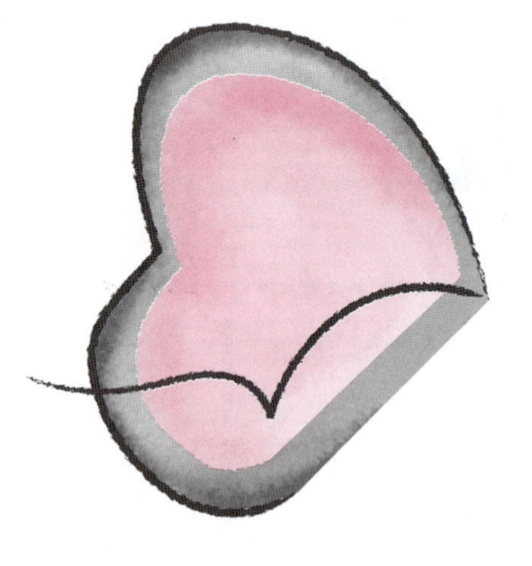
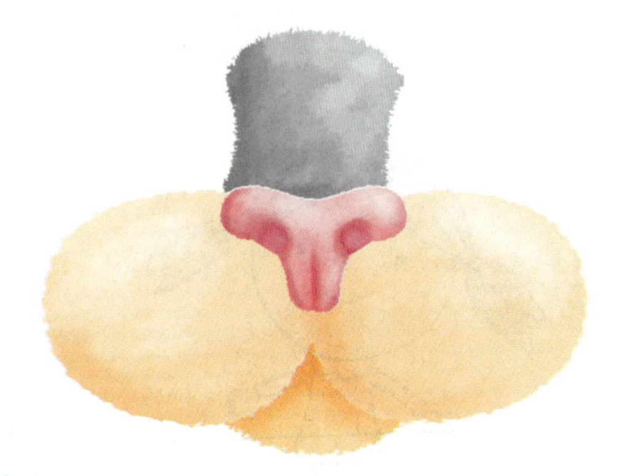

Objectives: Understand a story.

Complete the picture. 

What is under the elephant? Finger paint the eggs. 

● Color. Red for big. Yellow for small. 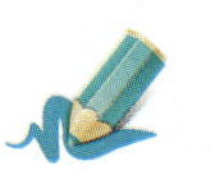

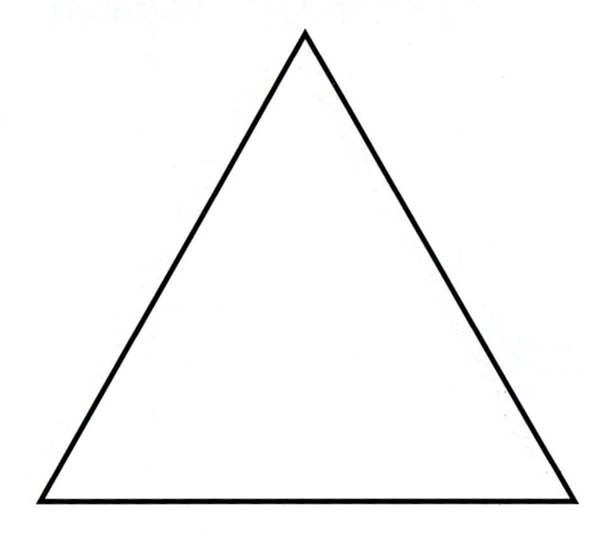

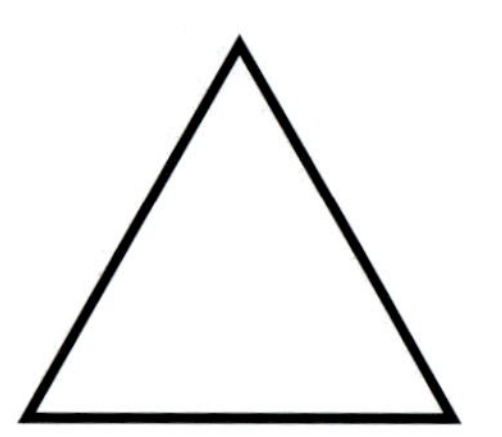

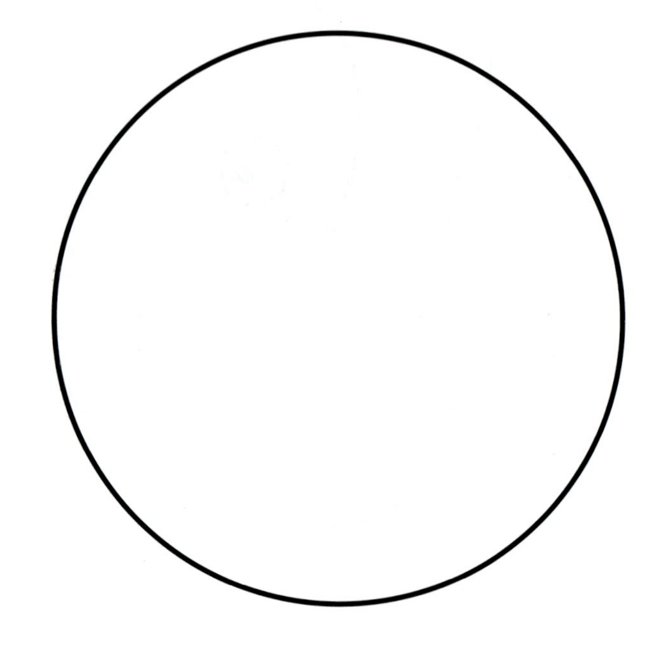

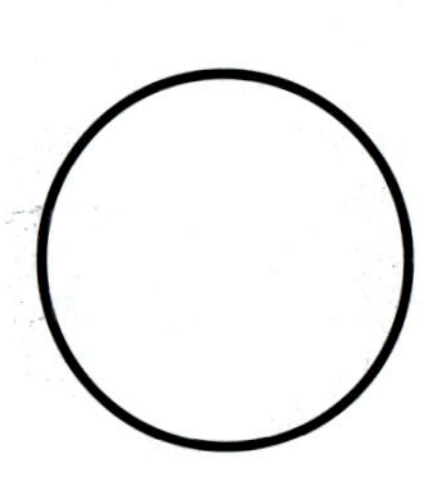

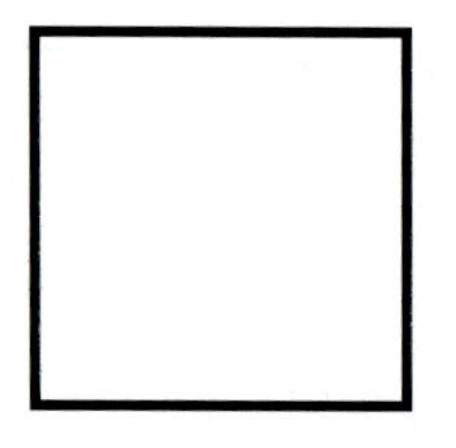

Objectives: Name shapes and identify big and small.

Follow your teacher's instructions. Circle the fingers and toes.

Think!
How many fingers and toes do you have?

Objectives: Say parts of the head and body. Touch.

Mark the mistakes with an X in picture 1.
Complete picture 2 with cutouts.

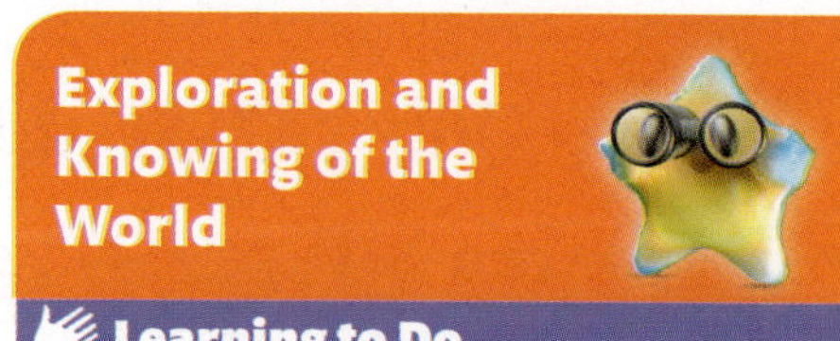
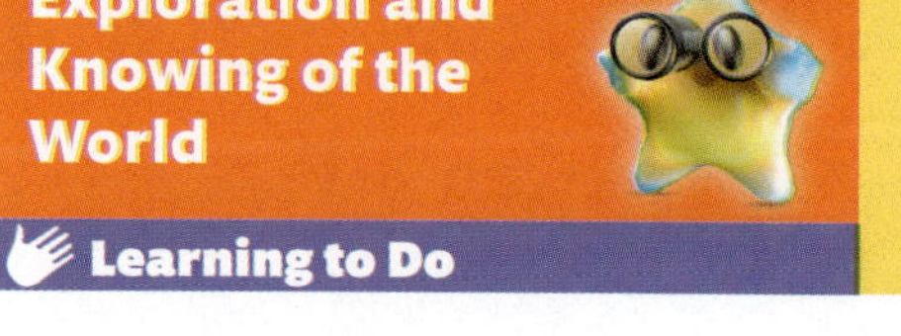

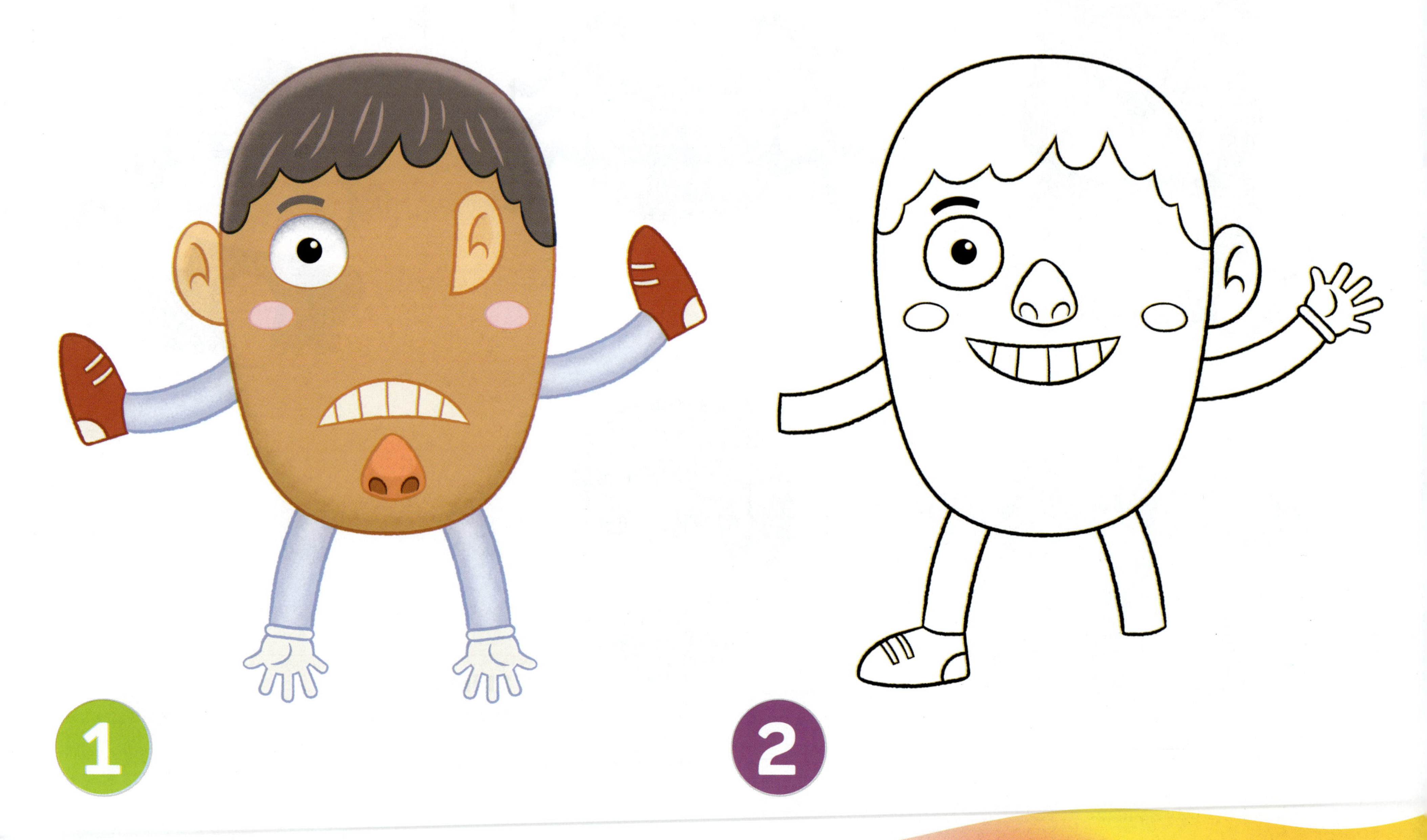

Objectives: Recognize symmetry in the body.

How do they feel? Color happy or sad.

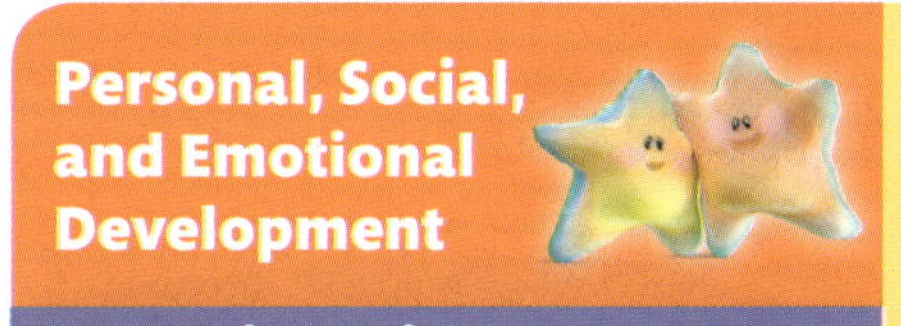

Draw how you feel today.

Objectives: Express emotions and feelings.

Listen. Circle why the rabbit loses.  

Think!
Why does the turtle win the race?

Tell a friend the story. 

Objectives: Understand a story.

Put the hen and elephant in their houses. Circle the big house.

Objectives: Short /e/ sound. Identify big and small.

Cut and paste. Say the shapes you know.

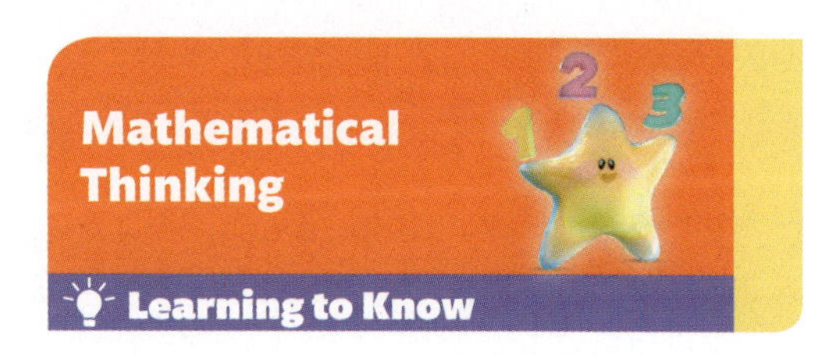

Objectives: Sort shapes with straight and curved lines.

Look at the pictures.
Circle  or . 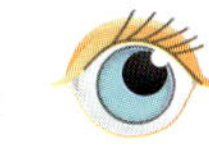 

What do they need? Look and match.

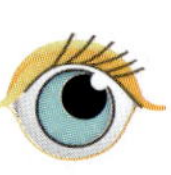

Exploration and Knowing of the World

Learning to Do

Think!
What do you need to draw a picture?

Objectives: Identify everyday objects and what they are for.

Listen. Check the first and the last picture.

Color how Sam feels.

Think!
Do you put your toys away when you finish playing?

Objectives: Follow rules.

Unit 3 What is a family?

- How many grandparents do you have?

- Listen. Match the pictures to the names. Circle the mom and dad. 38

- Listen to the chant and say it.

Objectives: Understand and retell a story.

Color the pictures of words with *i*.

41

Where does Nick live?

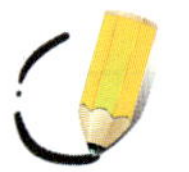

Objectives: Short /i/ sound.

Say. Cut and paste.   

Objectives: Match objects and numbers to 4.

Listen. Circle Isobel's brother and pet. 42

Language Instruction and Communication

Learning to Know

Think!
How many brothers and sisters do you have?

What is her pet's name?

Objectives: Learn the words for family members.

Look and circle what is the same. 

Exploration and Knowing of the World 

Learning to Do

Think!
How are families different?

Who do you look like? Draw. 

Objectives: Learn about different types of families.

Listen. Circle the people they mention. 43

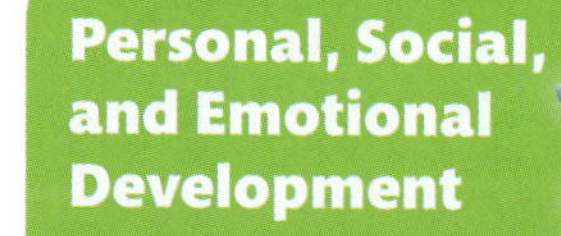

Personal, Social, and Emotional Development

Learning to Live Together
Learning to Live with Others

Think!
What do you like to do with your grandparents?

Talk about the families.

Objectives: Identify family members.

Listen.Circle the twins and Ivan. 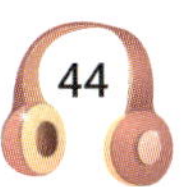 

Color the small family. How many do you see? 

Objectives: Understand and retell a story.

Draw something with an /i/ sound. Tell a friend.

Objectives: Short /i/ sound.

Color TALL. Circle SHORT. 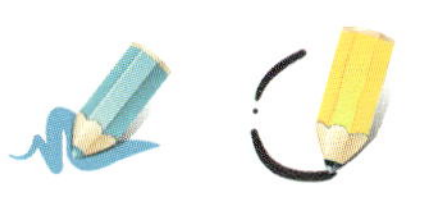

Mathematical Thinking

Learning to Know

Think!
Who is tall / short in your family?

Objectives: Identify tall and short.

- **Draw an animal that you like in the green circle. Draw an animal that you don't like in the yellow circle.**

Language Instruction and Communication

Learning to Know

- **Draw a family member in the red square.** 

Objectives: Learn and use the words for shapes and colors.

Listen and match. 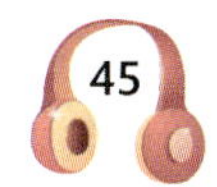 

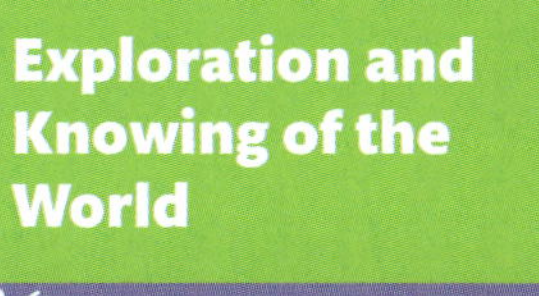

Think!
What do your mom and dad do?

What's your family like? Tell a friend. 

Objectives: Learn about different kinds of families.

Draw a star on the family that is most like yours. Say.

Personal, Social, and Emotional Development

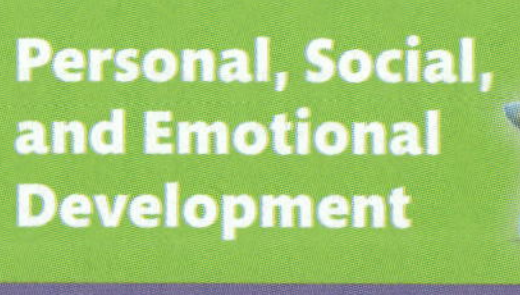

Learning to Live Together
Learning to Live with Others

Think!
Who do you live with?

Objectives: Identify family members.

Listen and number. Act out the story. 47

Objectives: Understand and retell a story.

Listen. Connect the pictures that have an /i/ sound to the letter.

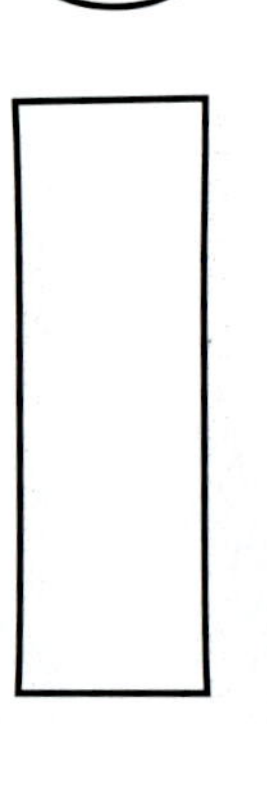

Color the *i*.

Objectives: Short /i/ sound.

Continue the pattern.

Objectives: Extend a simple pattern.

Tell the story using the pictures. 

I ❤

I ❤

I ❤

I ❤

Draw something you don't like.

Objectives: Likes and dislikes.

- Listen. Trace the letter *i*. 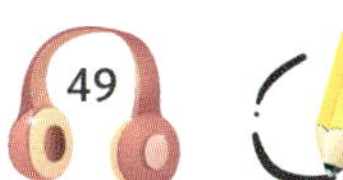 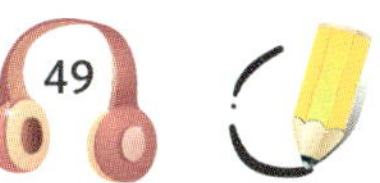

Exploration and Knowing of the World

Learning to Do

The Inuit

- Color the boy, igloo, and animals. 

Objectives: Learn about different kinds of families.

Circle the good actions. Cross out the bad actions.

Personal, Social, and Emotional Development

Learning to Live Together
Learning to Live with Others

Think!
What good actions do you do?

Objectives: Accept and follow rules.

Draw the missing faces. Listen and sing.

50

Objectives: Understand and retell a story.

Listen and guess what it is. 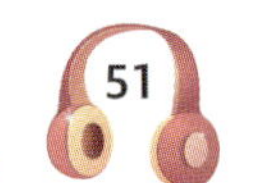

Connect the dots to find out.

Objectives: Short /i/ sound.

Sort the people. Cut and paste.

Mathematical Thinking

Learning to Know

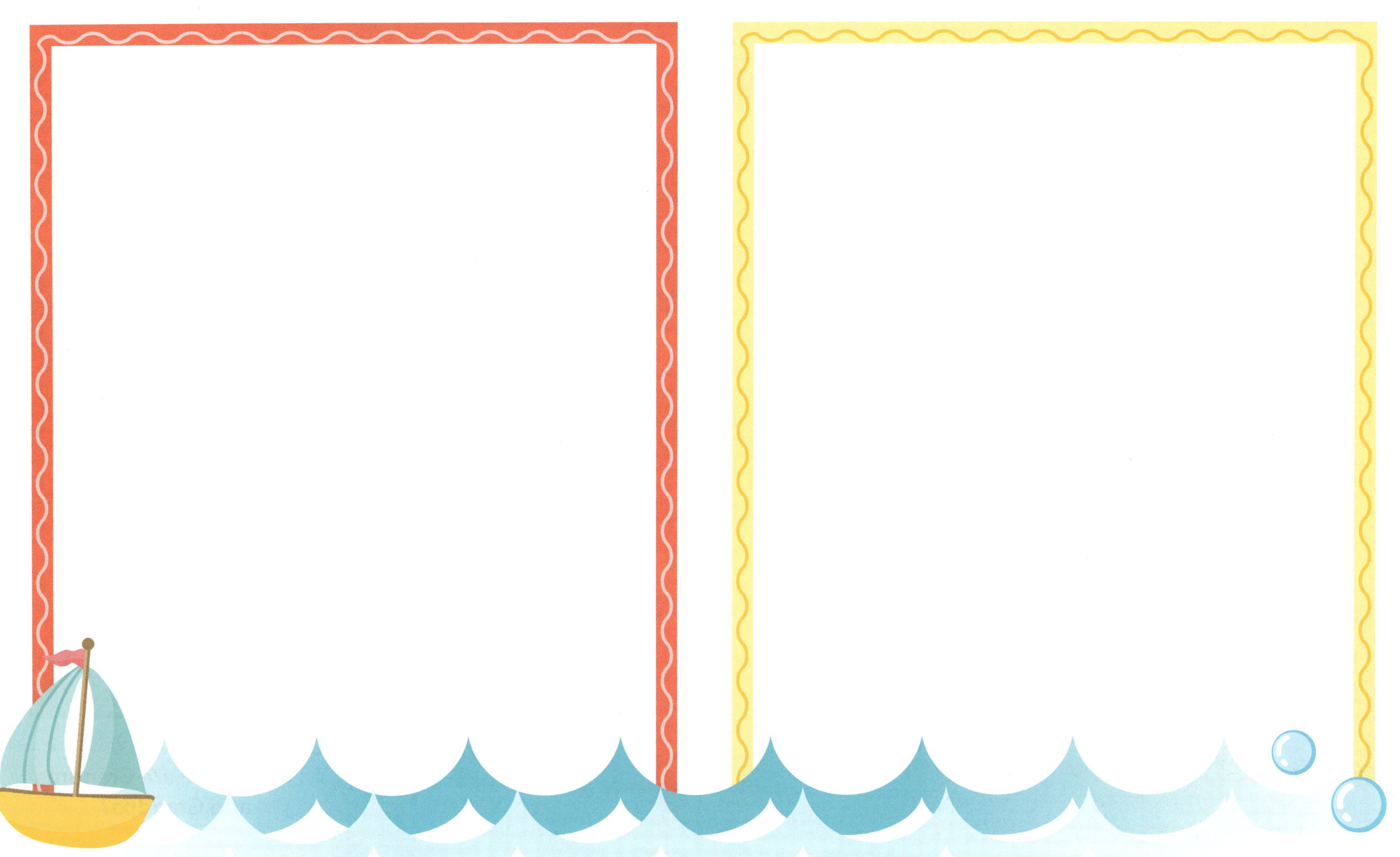

Objectives: Sort objects using one characteristic.

Listen and find. Draw the missing pictures. Talk about the picture.

Language Instruction and Communication

Learning to Know

Objectives: Learn the words for family members.

Listen. Find the right family and circle. Talk about the pictures.

Objectives: Learn about different kinds of families.

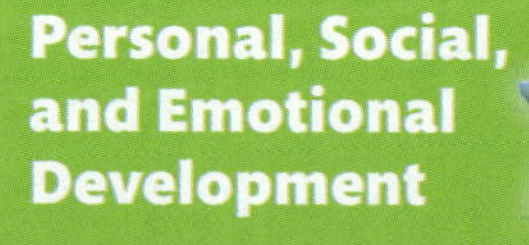

Personal, Social, and Emotional Development

Learning to Live Together
Learning to Live with Others

Are you a good family member? Color the right face.

Are you a good friend? Color the right face.

Objectives: Accept and follow rules.

Unit 4 Do you share your toys? Why?

Look and listen. Color the iguanas green.

Objectives: Listen to and understand a story.

Connect the pictures to the words. 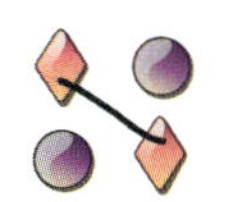

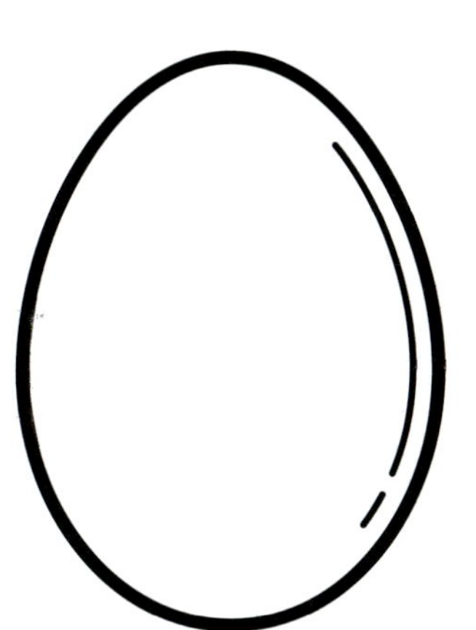

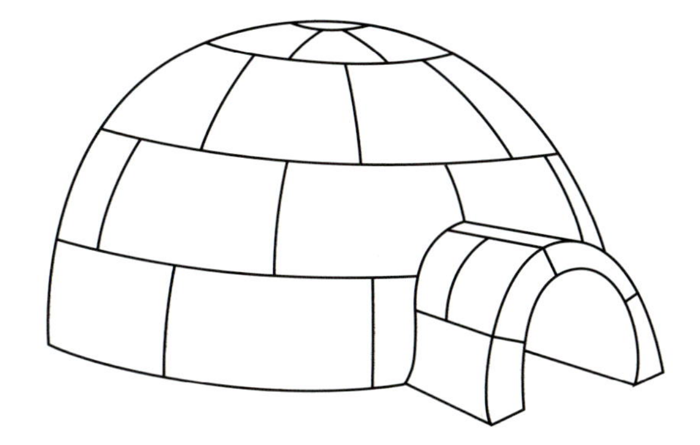

igloo

egg

ant

Objectives: Identify words with short /a/, /e/, and /i/ sounds.

Draw and color.

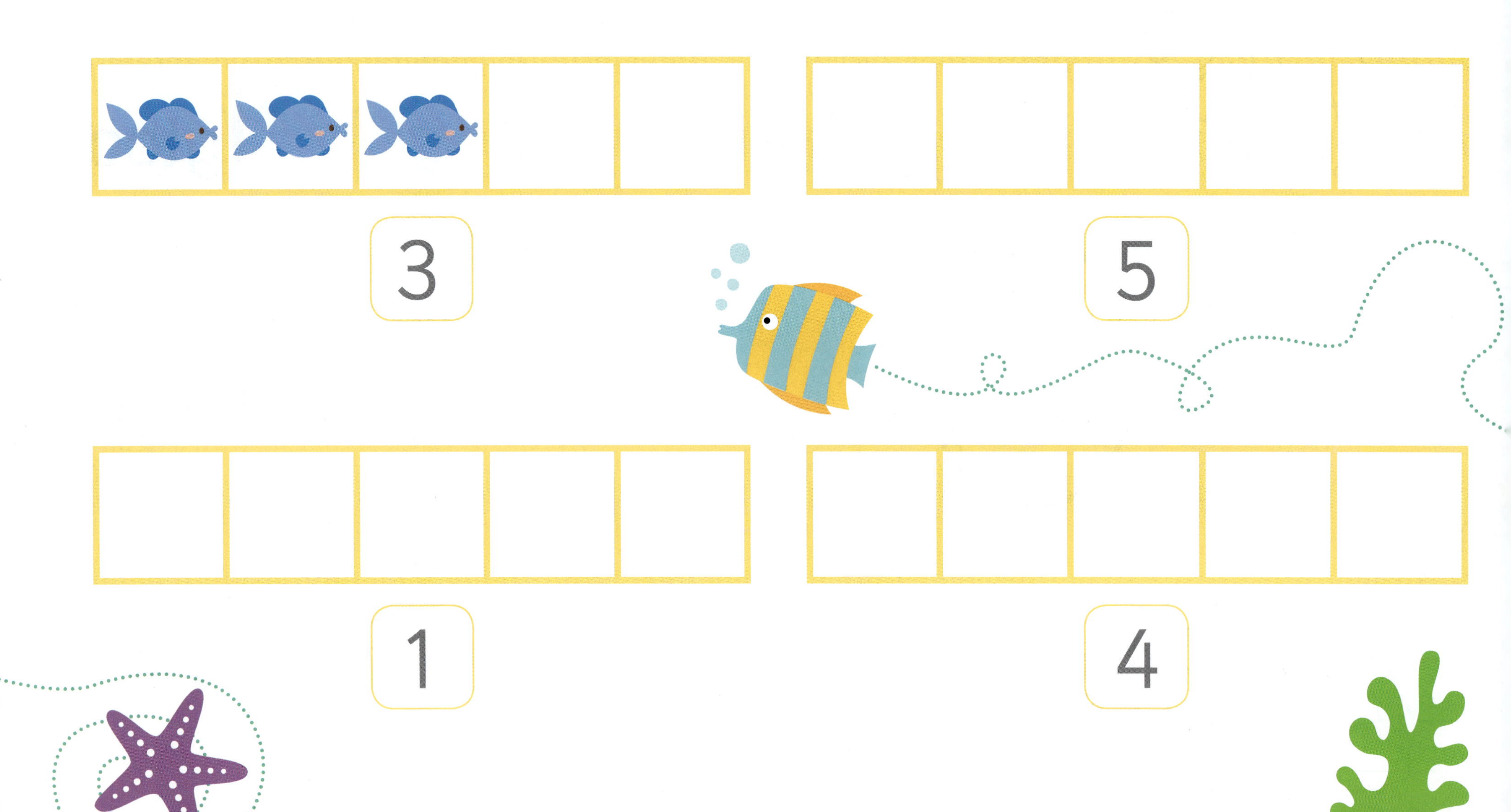

Objectives: Use a five-frame to show amounts to 5.

Put the toys in the box. Listen. 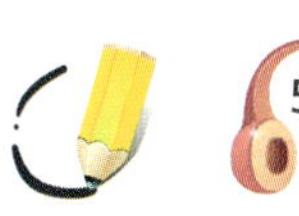 

Language Instruction and Communication

Learning to Know

What's your favorite toy?

Objectives: Learn words for toys.

Talk about the pictures. Trace the numbers.

Exploration and Knowing of the World

Learning to Do

2

Think!
Is there a game like this in your country?

Objectives: Develop social awareness.

Listen. Circle Sammy's car. Act out the scene.

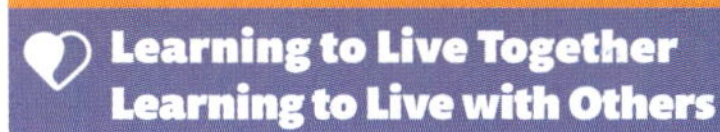

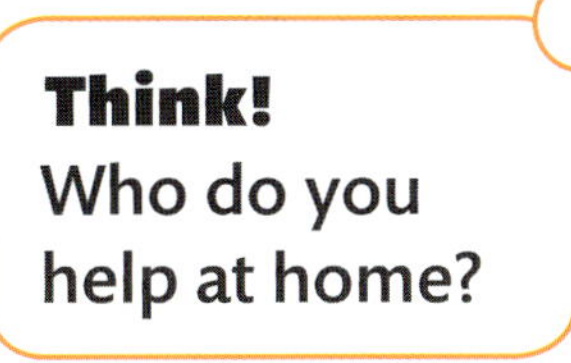

Objectives: Interact with others.

Listen. Tell the story. Circle the big *A*'s and the small *a*'s.

Albert

car

plane

Albert

Objectives: Listen to and understand a story.

Color the elephant blue, the ant red and the iguana yellow.

Which picture do you like?

Objectives: Identify words with short /a/, /e/, and /i/ sounds.

Point and say. Trace 5 times.

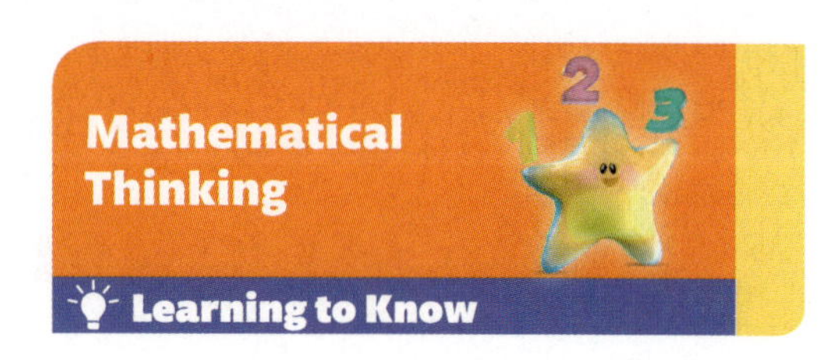

Objectives: Trace numbers 1 and 2.

Draw and match. Say the words.  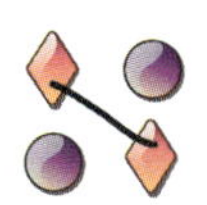 

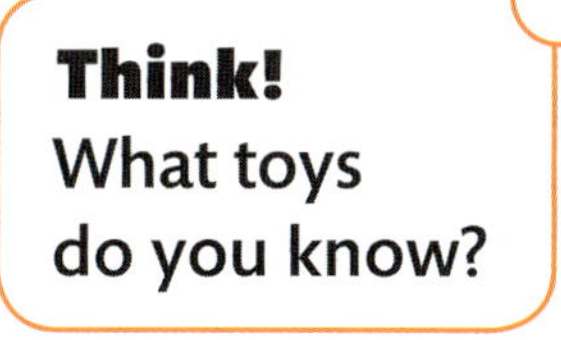

Objectives: Learn words for toys.

Paste the cutouts. Draw 3 more toys. Listen and play.

Toy Bingo!

Objectives: Play games.

Look. Tell the story. Circle.

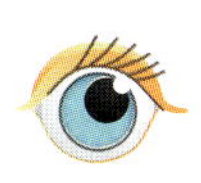

Personal, Social, and Emotional Development

Learning to Live Together
Learning to Live with Others

Think!
How can you be kind to others?

Listen and say. 62

Objectives: Interact with others.

Listen. How old is Penny today? Count her presents. 63

Draw the presents under the correct number.

1

2

3

4

Objectives: Listen to and understand a story.

Trace the letters. Say the sounds.  

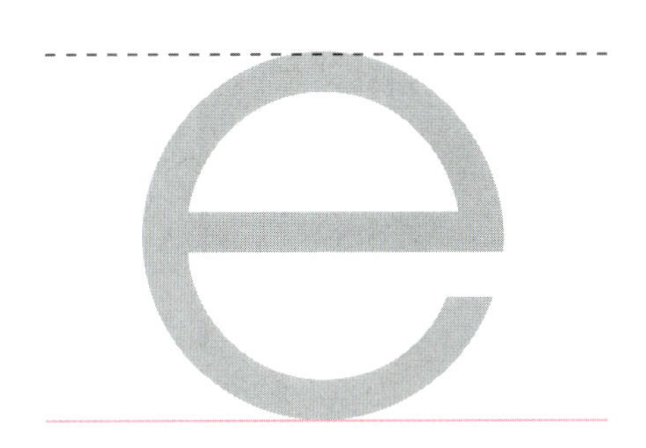

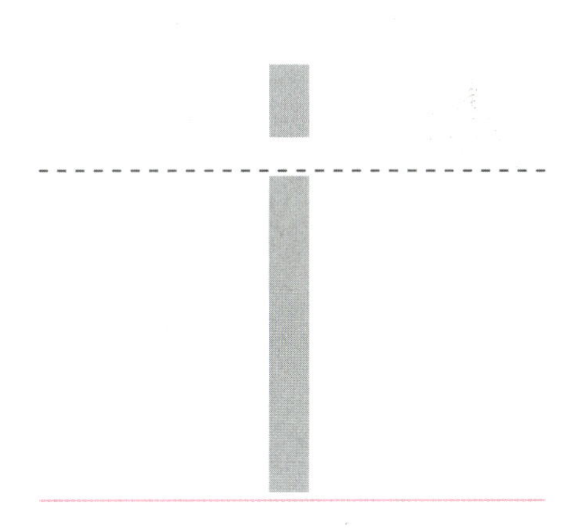

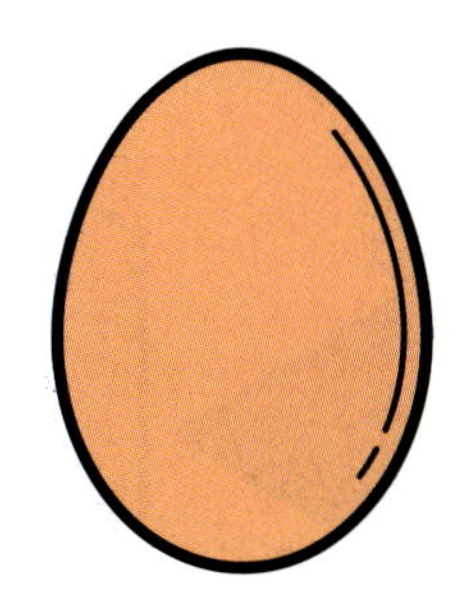

Say words that begin with these sounds. 

Objectives: identify words with short /a/, /e/, and /i/ sounds.

Point, say, and color.

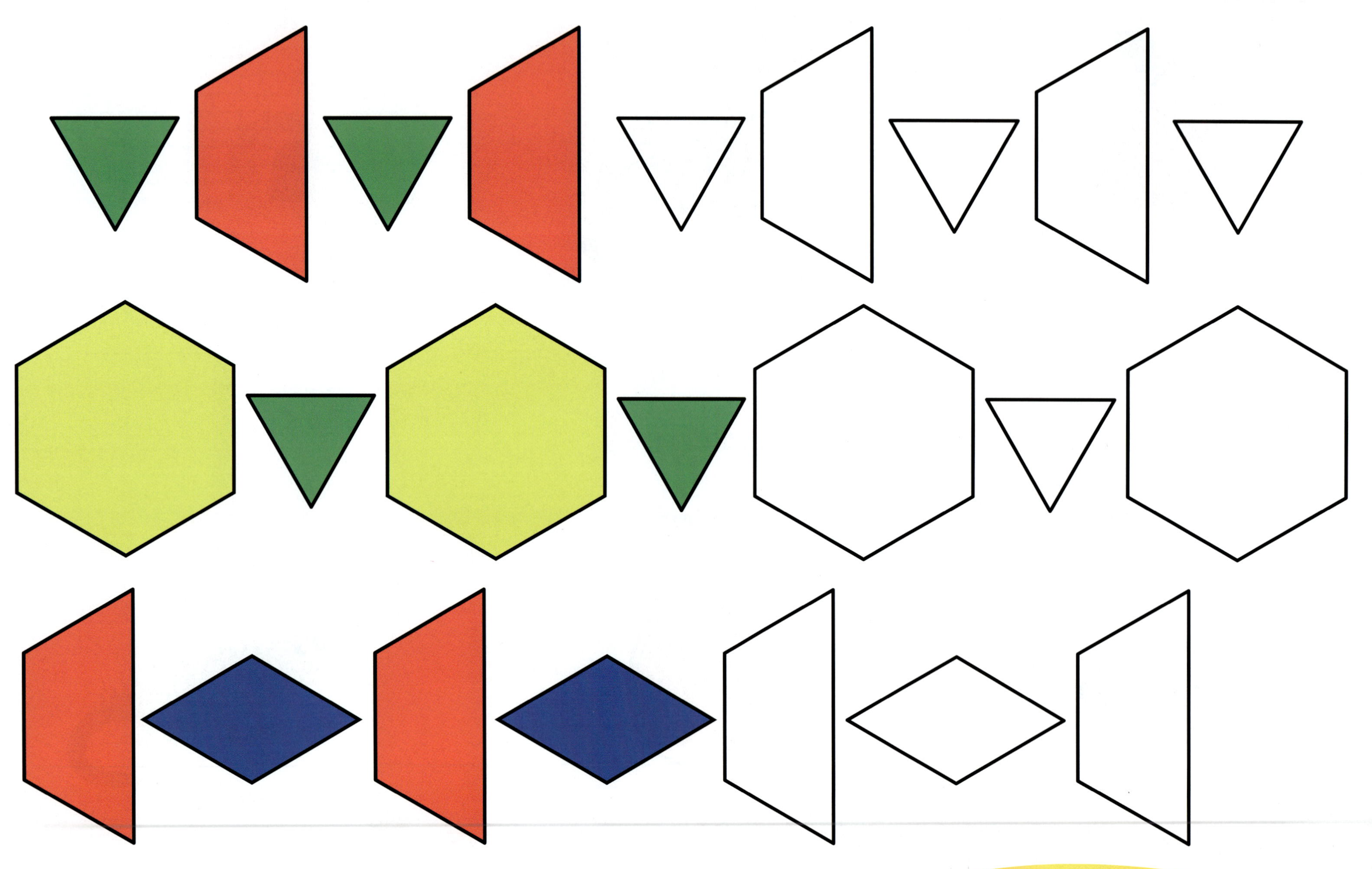

Objectives: Extend a pattern.

Add pictures to the *a*, *e*, and *i* boxes.

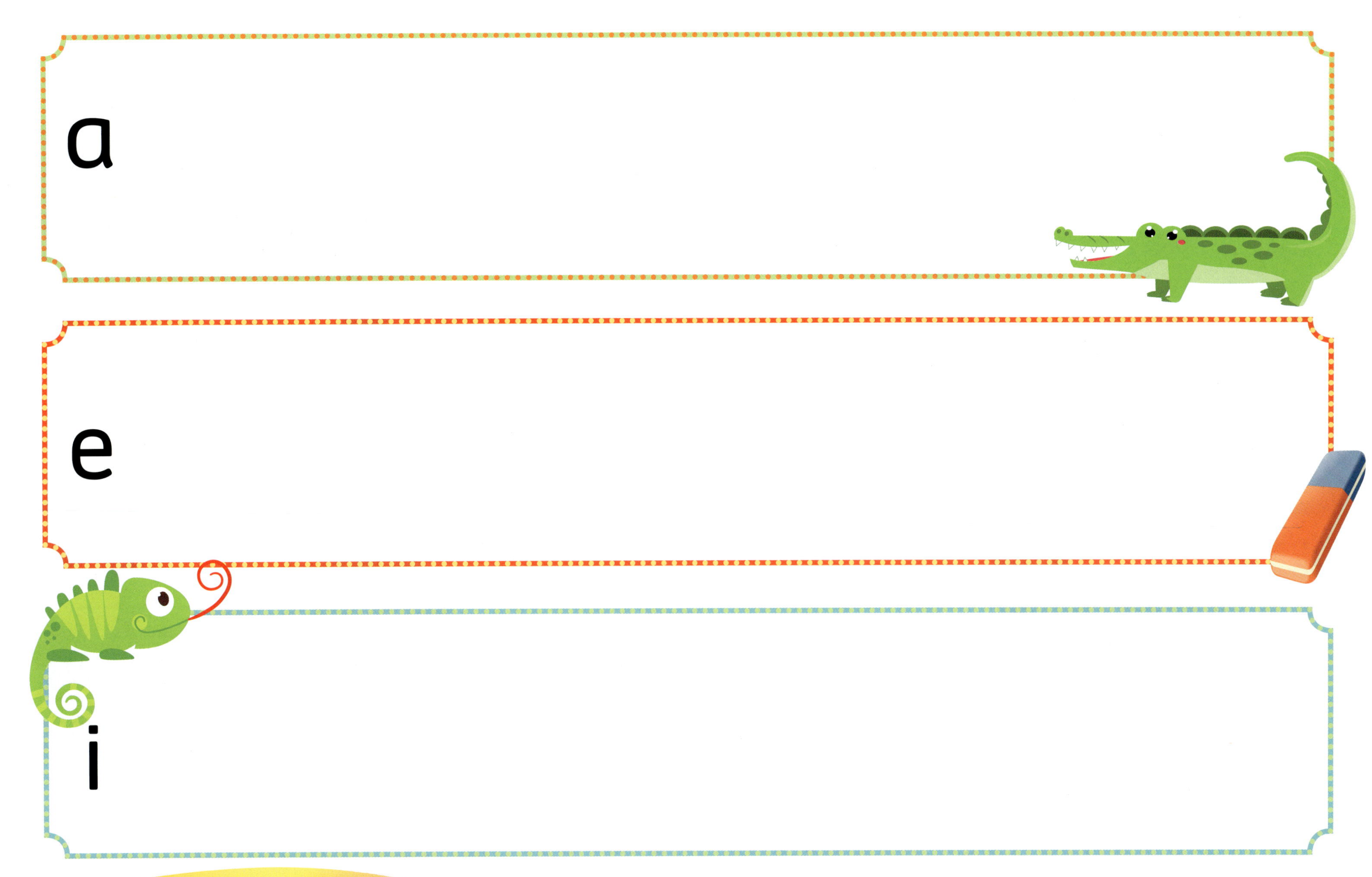

Objectives: Vowels.

Look, listen, and solve the riddles. Trace and match the numbers with the pictures.

1

2

3

4

Make sentences about the pictures.

Objectives: Play games.

What are the children doing? 

Think!
How do you feel when someone shares with you?

Draw another play-together toy.

Objectives: Share toys.

Listen to the story. Circle *i*, *A*, and *E*. Tell the story. 65

Edgar and Abby

Objectives: Listen to and understand a story.

Circle the letters *a*, *e*, and *i*.

Objectives: Identify words with short /a/, /e/, and /i/ sounds.

Color LONG. Cross out SHORT.  

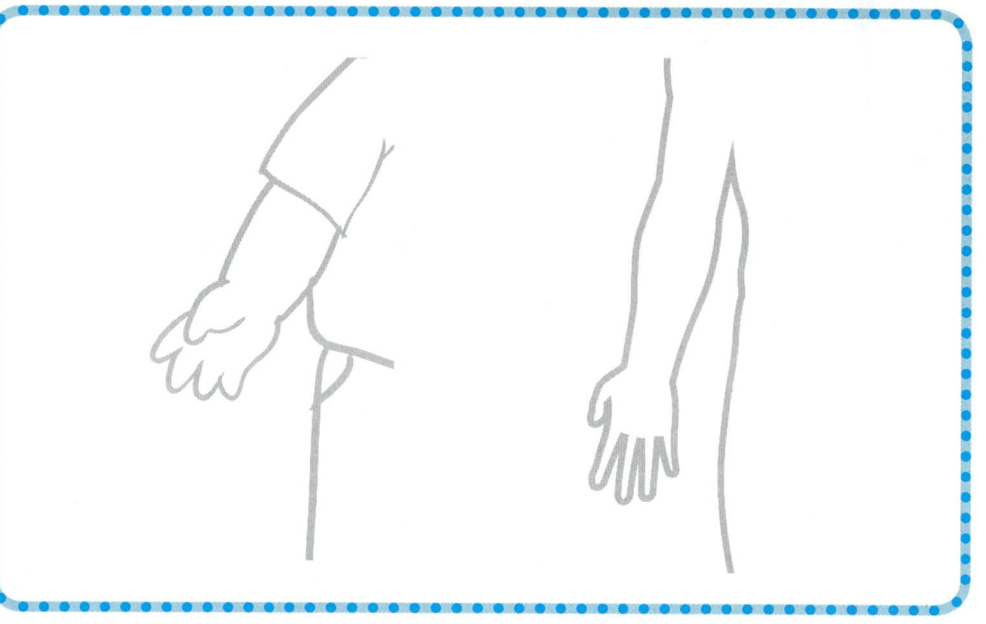

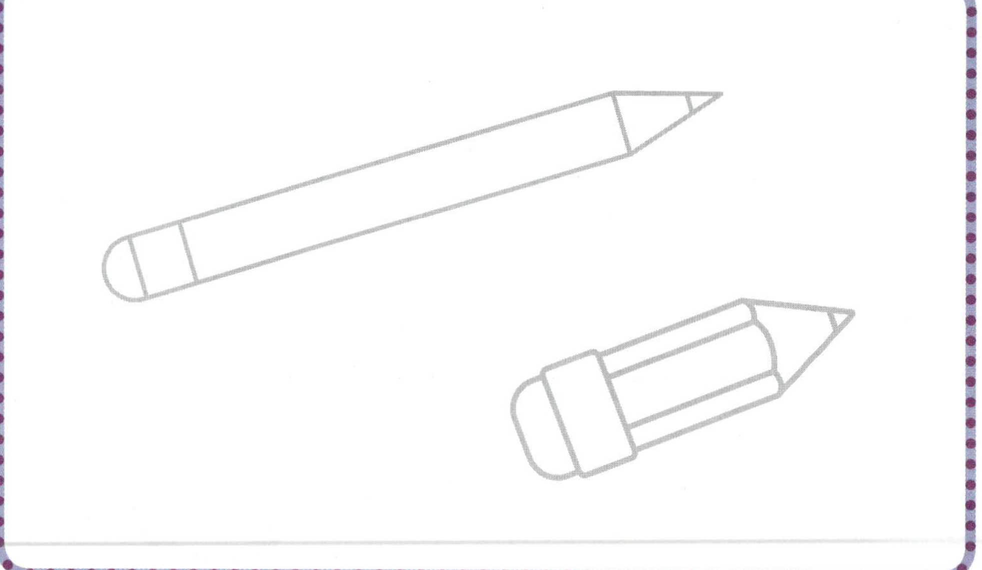

Objectives: Identify long and short.

Say the words. Circle the big toys in red. Circle the small toys in blue.

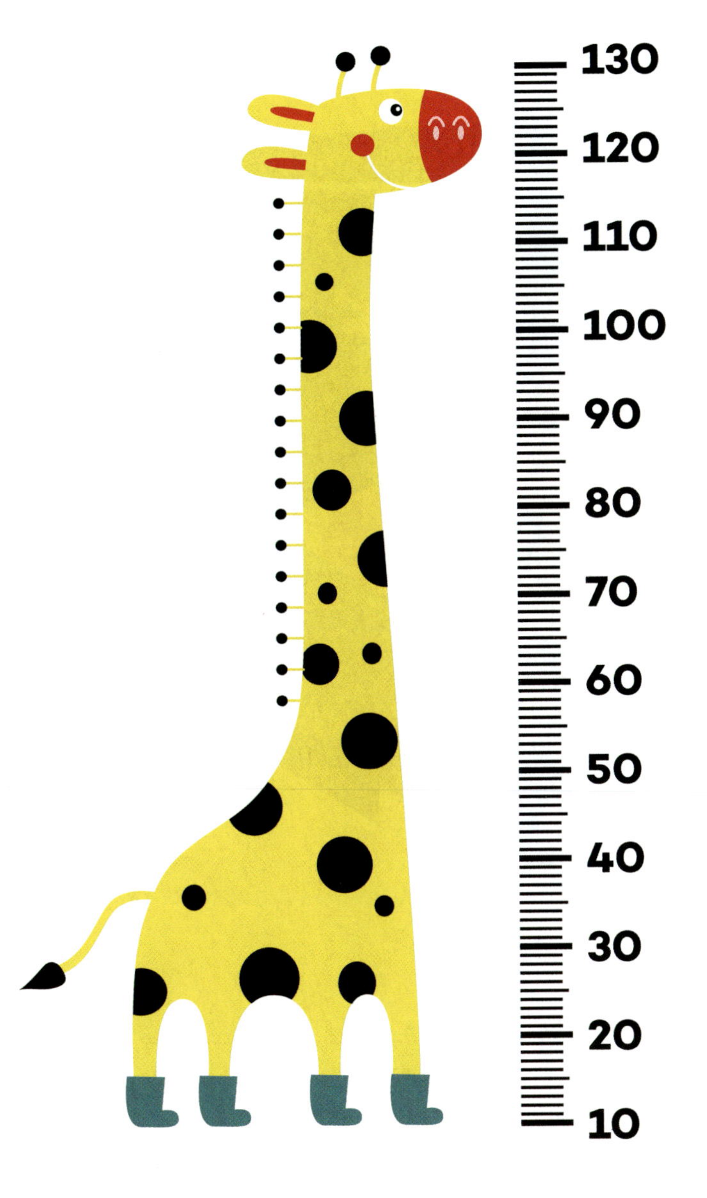

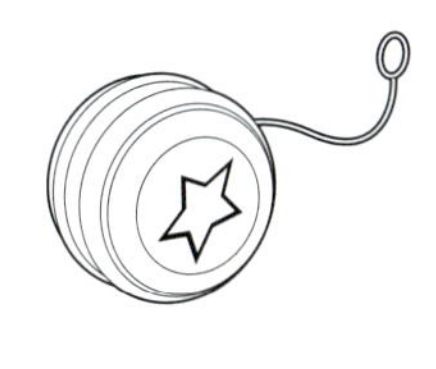

Listen and say.

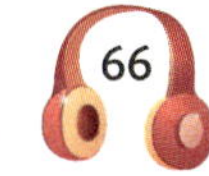

Objectives: Describe objects according to size, shape, and color.

Listen and sing. 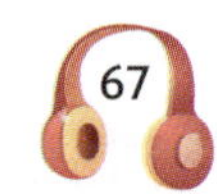 

Think!
Why is it important to give your old toys to others?

Objectives: Develop social awareness of oneself and objects.

Check the toys you like to play with. 

Count the toys you like playing with. Circle the number. 

1 2 3 4 5 6

Objectives: Interact with others.

Listen and find the children's toys. Circle. What's different about the toys?

69

Objectives: Listen to and understand a story.

Trace. Say your favorite *a*, *e*, or *i* word.

Apple begins with a a a.

Egg begins with e e e.

Iguana begins with i i i.

Objectives: Identify words with short /a/, /e/, and /i/ sounds.

Point and say. Cut and paste.

Objectives: Sort objects.

Trace the shapes. Match the objects to the words.

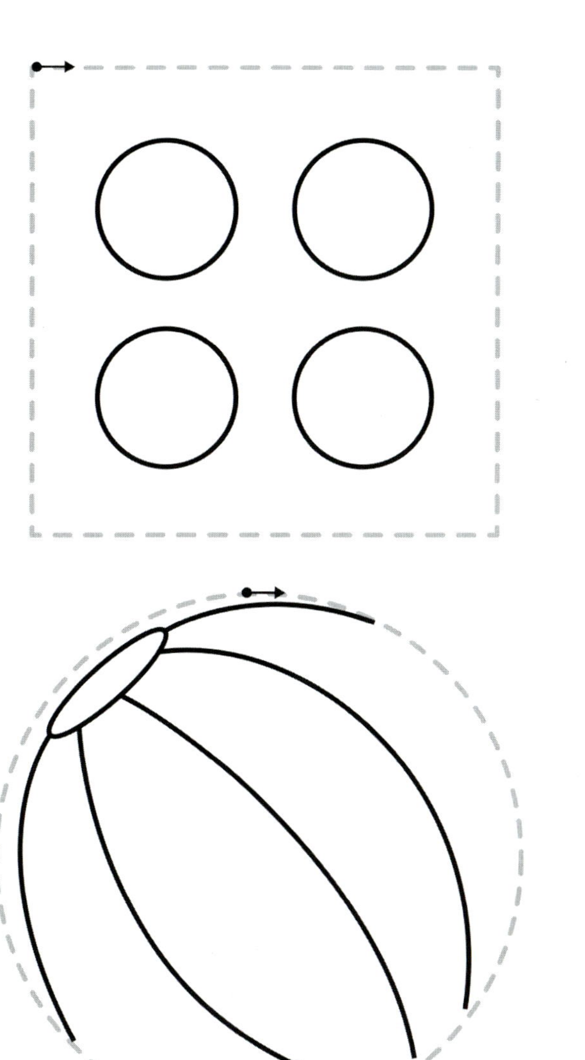

school

toys

Objectives: Describe objects according to size, shape, and color.

Talk about the shapes.

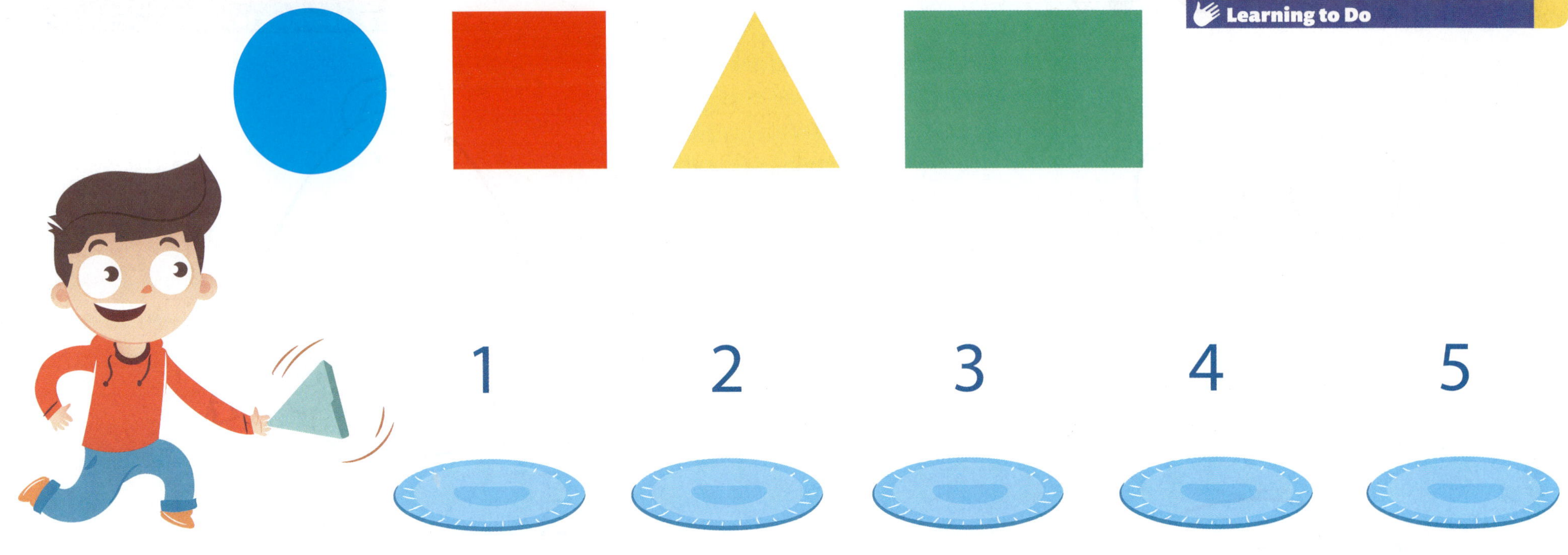

Make a beanbag. Play a beanbag game!

Objectives: Play games.

● What are the children doing? Look and circle a book that you like.

Think!
What's your favorite story?

● Draw your favorite book cover.

Objectives: Interact with others.

Listen. Color the drum.
Draw the last picture. 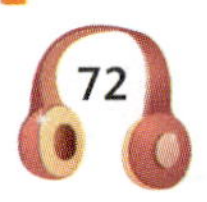 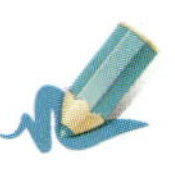 

Objectives: Listen to and understand a story.

Draw a triangle around the ant, a square around the elephant and a circle around the igloo.

Objectives: Identify words with short /a/, /e/, and /i/ sounds.
Shapes.

Count, color, and match.  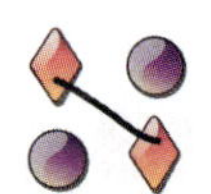

4

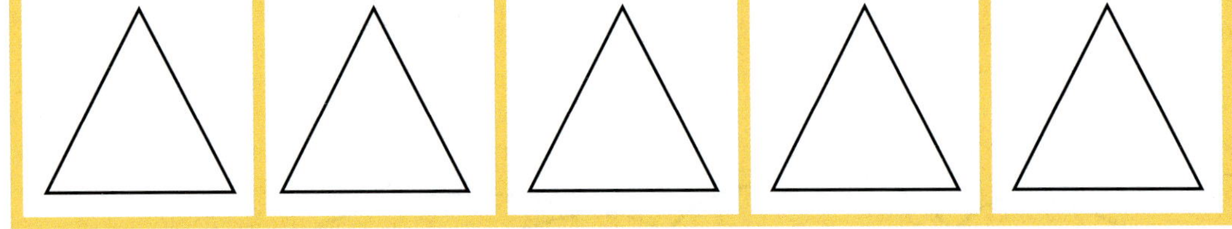

2

5

3

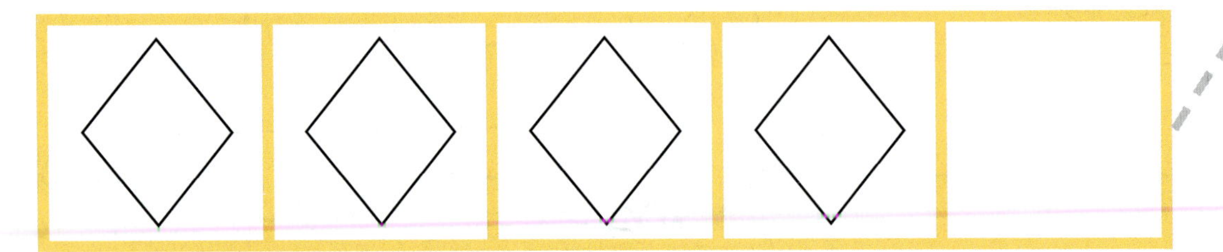

Objectives: Count up to 5.

Listen. Trace the letters and match. 74

Think!
What other things do you like to do?

Now, listen and chant. 75

Objectives: Vowels.

What are they saying? Complete the scribble. 76

Objectives: Play games.

Personal, Social, and Emotional Development

Learning to Live Together
Learning to Live with Others

Circle the picture where the girl is kind.

Underline the right sentence in red.

It's good to play together.

It's bad to play together.

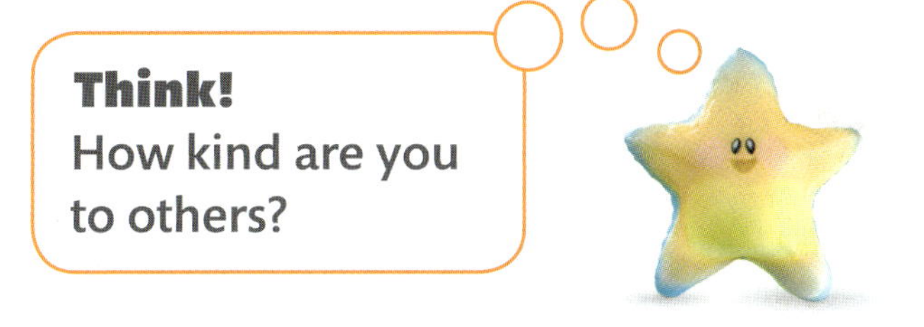

Objectives: Interact with others.

Unit 5 How do you help at home?

Listen to the story. Circle the *o*'s.  

Otto and the Orange Juice

Objectives: Understand and retell a story.

Circle the big octopus. Color the small octopus.

Objectives: Short /o/ sound. Identify big and small.

Count, trace, and color.

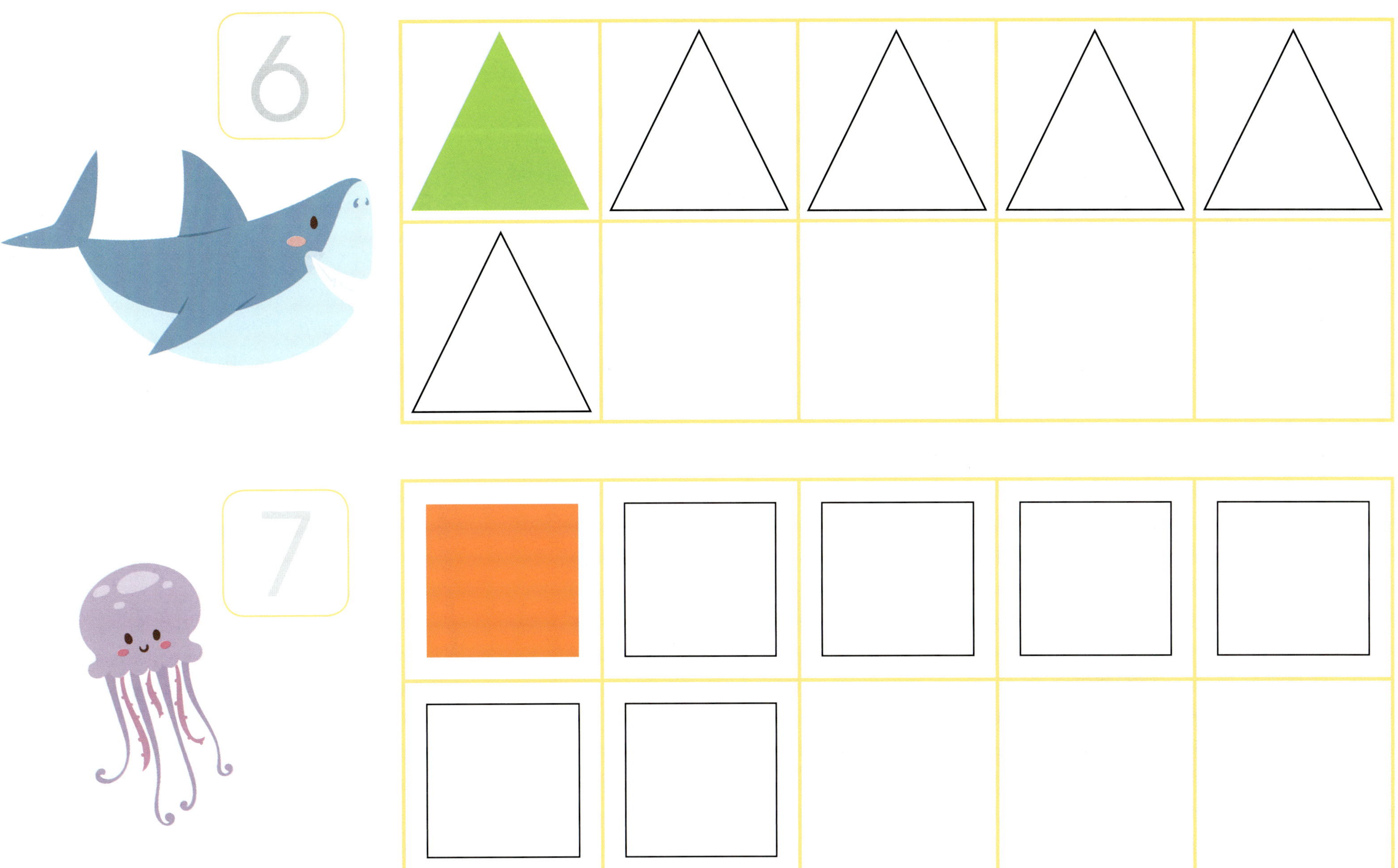

Objectives: Match numbers with objects up to 7.

How can you help at home? Color the letters you know.

toys

clothes

What can't you do because it's dangerous? Draw.

stove

apple

Think!
What chores do you do at home?

Objectives: Talk about chores they can or can't do.

Talk about Kalifa. 

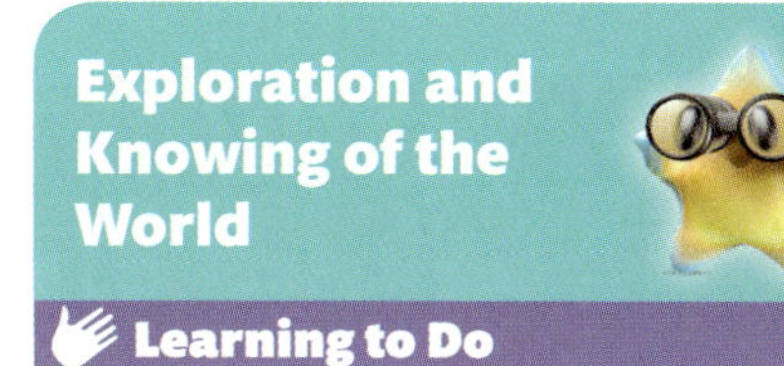

Where do you dry your clothes? Draw. 

Think!
Where do you wash your clothes?

Objectives: Talk about different houses.

Do you make your own bed? Listen and order the pictures.

Personal, Social, and Emotional Development

Learning to Live Together
Learning to Live with Others

What toys do you sleep with?

Objectives: Talk about their homes and chores.

Listen to the story. Tell a classmate.
Circle the *o*'s. 81

Olivia's Broom

Objectives: Understand and retell a story.

Listen. Find the ostrich. Circle. 82

Phonemic Awareness

Learning to Know

Objectives: Short /o/ sound.

Point, say, and trace.

Objectives: Trace numbers 3 and 4. Identify heavy and light.

Where are the footprints? Color and say.

Where's the dog? Circle.

Objectives: Rooms in a house.

What's wrong? Circle. 

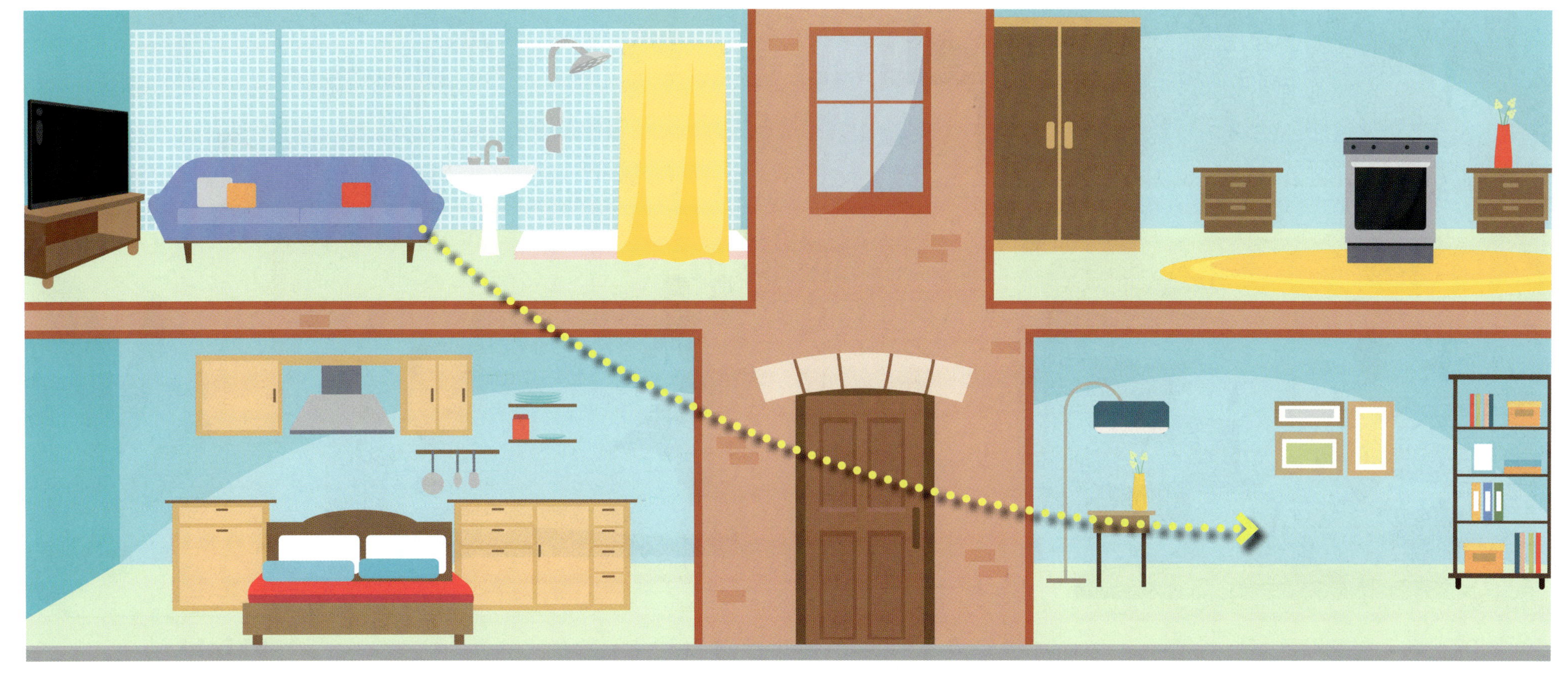

Put the objects in the correct room. 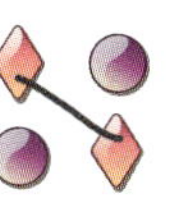

Objectives: Rooms in a house.

Check the chores you do. Cross out the chores you don't do. ✓ X

Personal, Social, and Emotional Development

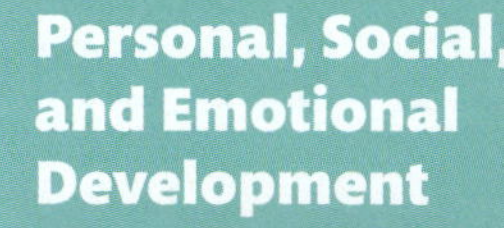

Learning to Live Together
Learning to Live with Others

Think!
What chores don't you like to do?

Compare with a friend.

Objectives: Talk about their homes and chores.

Listen to the story. 

Check the chores the children have to do.  

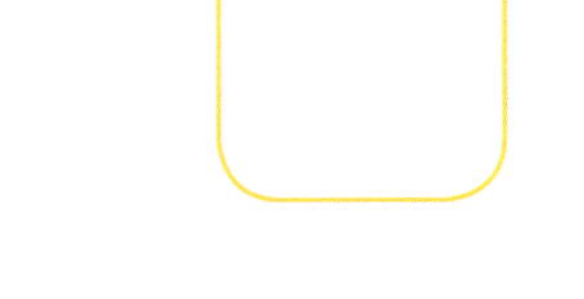

Objectives: Understand and retell a story.

Listen. Color and trace.  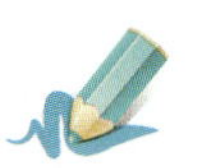 

otter

orange

Objectives: Short /o/ sound.

Point, say, cut, and paste.

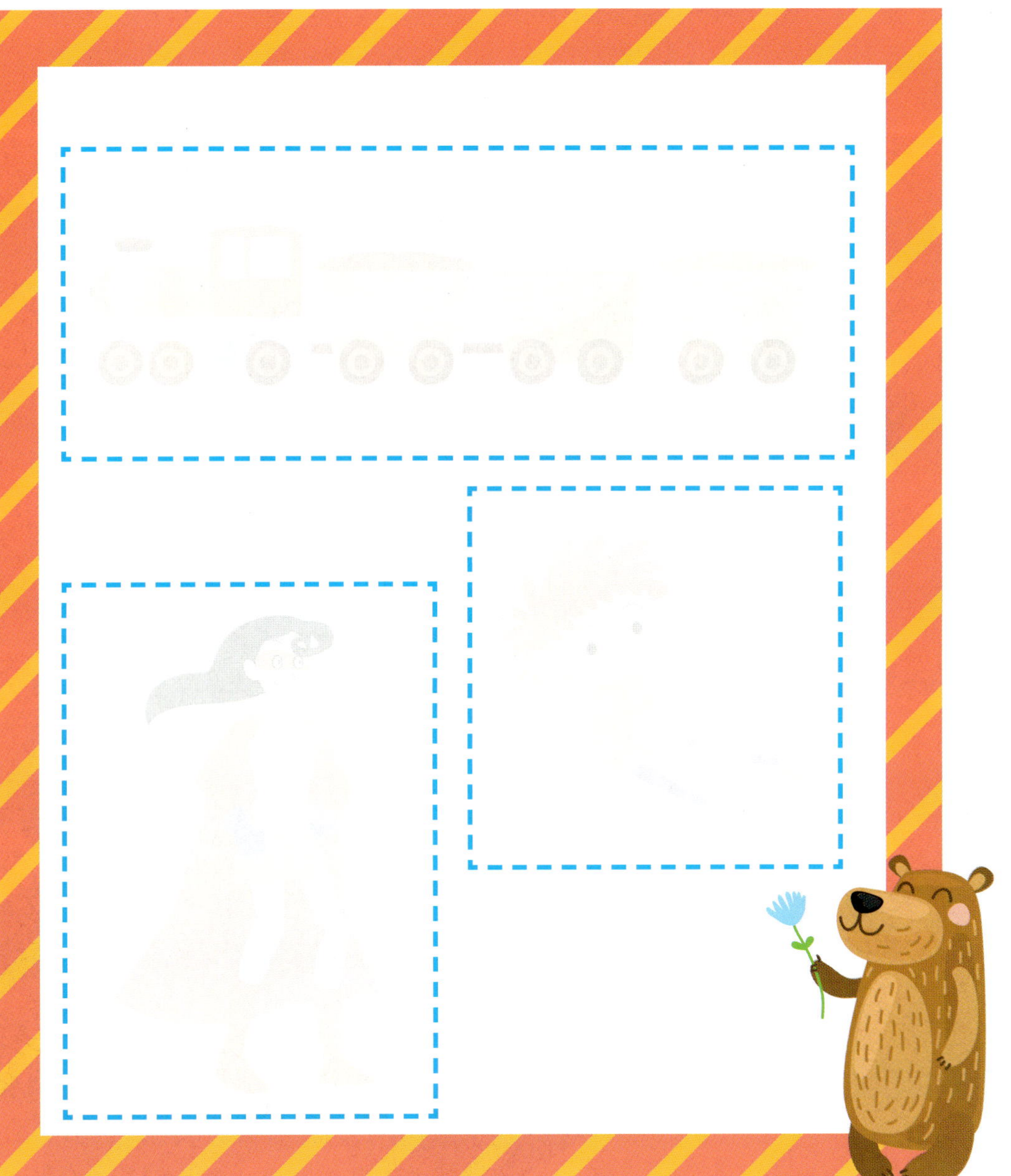

Objectives: Sort objects.

Listen to the story of the Little Red Hen. Circle the dog's answer.

Objectives: Understand and answer questions.

Why is water important? 

What can you do to save water? Circle.

Objectives: Follow rules to conserve water.

Talk about the pictures. Act out the situations.

Think!
What chore is fun to do?

Draw what you do to help at home.

Objectives: Accept and follow rules.

Listen and retell the story. 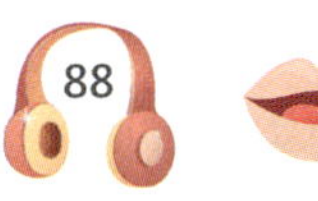 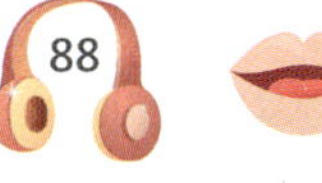

Literacy

Learning to Know

How does Oscar feel? Say.  

Objectives: Understand and retell a story.

Listen. Match BIG and small. 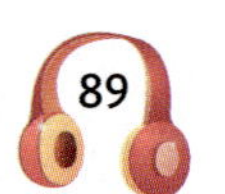 

small

What sound do the words begin with? 

Objectives: Short /o/ sound. Identify big and small.

Count, trace, and color.

Objectives: Match objects with numbers up to 9.

Where are the orange kittens? Listen. Color the kittens.

Draw the kittens on the bed.

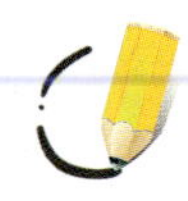

Objectives: Furniture. Prepositions *on, under.*

Listen and trace. 

germs

Draw a germ.

Think!
Why do we clean the house?

Objectives: Follow rules.

Check the correct pictures. Say.

Personal, Social, and Emotional Development

Learning to Live Together
Learning to Live with Others

Think!
Which is better, doing chores alone or together with your family? Why?

Objectives: Talk about chores.

Unit 6 How do you take care of your pet?

Listen to the story. Complete the picture and the dog's name. 93

Retell the story.

Objectives: Understand and retell a story.

Listen. Circle the *U*'s.  

Objectives: Short /u/ sound.

Mathematical Thinking
Learning to Know

Count, trace, and draw.

6

7

Objectives: Match objects and numbers up to 7.

Listen and find the pictures. Match the shapes to the animals.

Objectives: Use the words for shapes and colors.

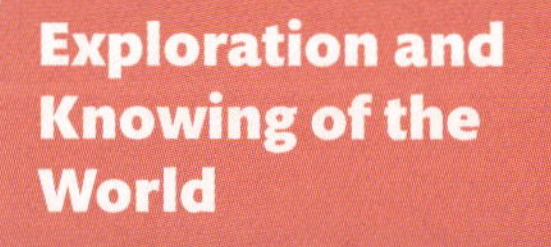

Where do they live? 

Match these animals to their habitats. 

Think!
What animals live in trees?

Objectives: Associate animals with their habitats.

Match the pets to what they need.

Objectives: Associate pets with homes.

Listen to the story. 97

Who saw Ulysses? Circle the correct picture.

Objectives: Understand and retell a story.

Color and trace. 

Objectives: Short /u/ sound.

Count, say, and trace.  

Mathematical Thinking

Learning to Know

5  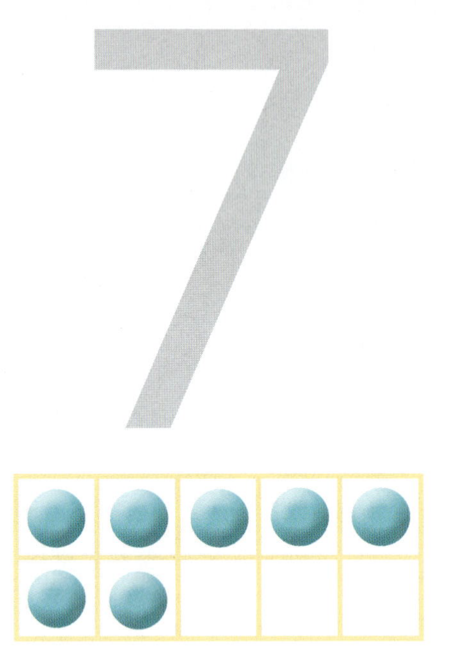

5 5 5 5 5 5 5 5 5 5 5

6 6 6 6 6 6 6 6 6 6 6

7 7 7 7 7 7 7 7 7 7 7

Objectives: Trace numbers 5, 6, and 7.

Talk about shapes and colors. 

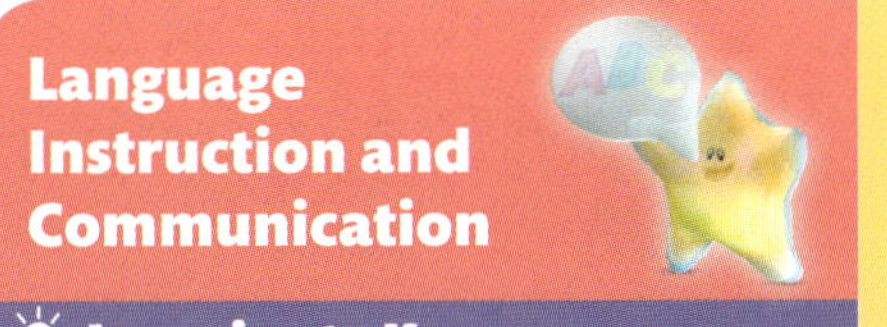

Complete the pattern. 

    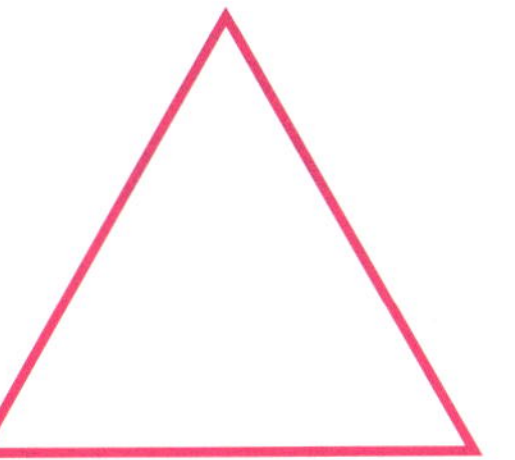 ______________

Objectives: Use words for shapes and colors.

How do these animals help us? 

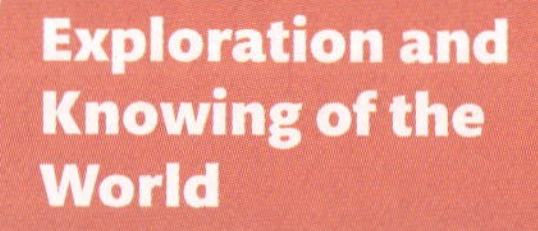

Draw another animal that helps us.

Objectives: Helping others.

Is everyone kind to animals? What do pets need?

What animal needs help? Circle.

Think!
How can you help animals?

Objectives: Recognize when someone needs help.

Find the *U* and color it. Color Ulster's toy, too.

Ulster

Listen. Circle who helps Cindy.  

Objectives: Understand and retell a story.

Listen. Match the pictures to the *u*. Trace.

Objectives: Short /u/ sound.

Point, cut, and paste.

First... Next... Then...

Objectives: Sequence simple events.

Say the animals.

What sound do pets make? Number.

Objectives: Learn the words for pets.

Are chimpanzees smart? Circle what they can do in the wild.

Think!
What other animal is smart?

Objectives: Talk about animals.

Listen and number the pictures. 

Objectives: Understanding commands.

Listen. Who's talking? Draw. 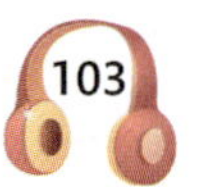 

It's Uriel!

Complete the name. 

Objectives: Understand and retell a story.

Listen. Draw a triangle around the *u* words. 105

sun

umbrella

cat

duck

Objectives: Short /u/ sound. Shapes.

Cut and paste by color.

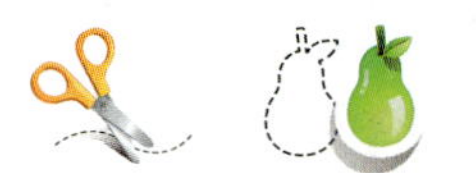

Objectives: Sort objects.

Listen and complete the picture. 

Objectives: Talk about belongings.

Listen. Match the moms and dads with their babies.

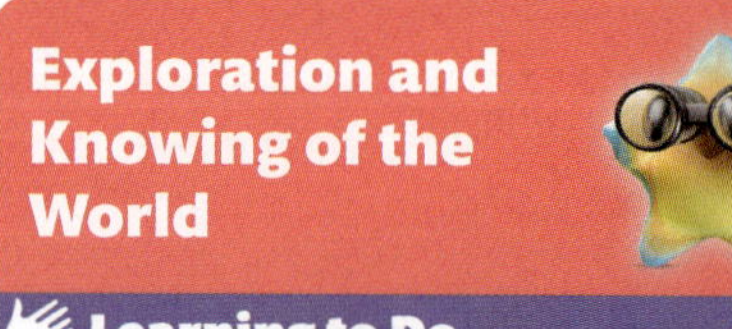

Think!
Who lives in the forest?

Objectives: Associate mother/father animals with their babies.

Listen, look, and number the pictures in the correct order.

Put the turtle back into the clean tank.

Objectives: Helping others.

- **Listen. Circle the food the bunny likes.** 109

The Hungry Bunny

- **Find the *u*'s and color them.**

Objectives: Understand and retell a story.

Draw a duck under the umbrella. 

Trace.

A duck under an umbrella.

Objectives: Short /u/ sound.

Point. Cut out and paste. Count the squares.

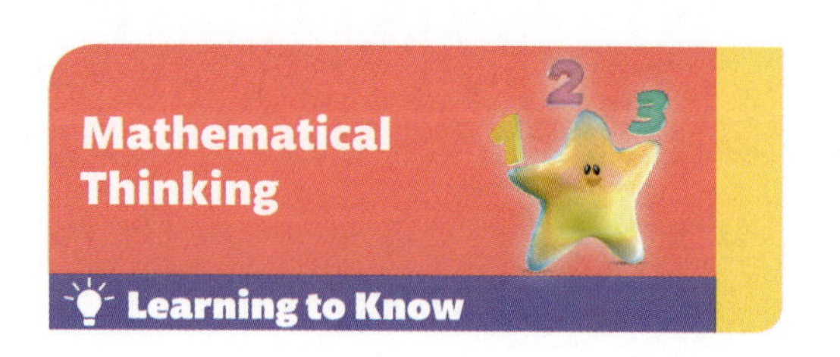

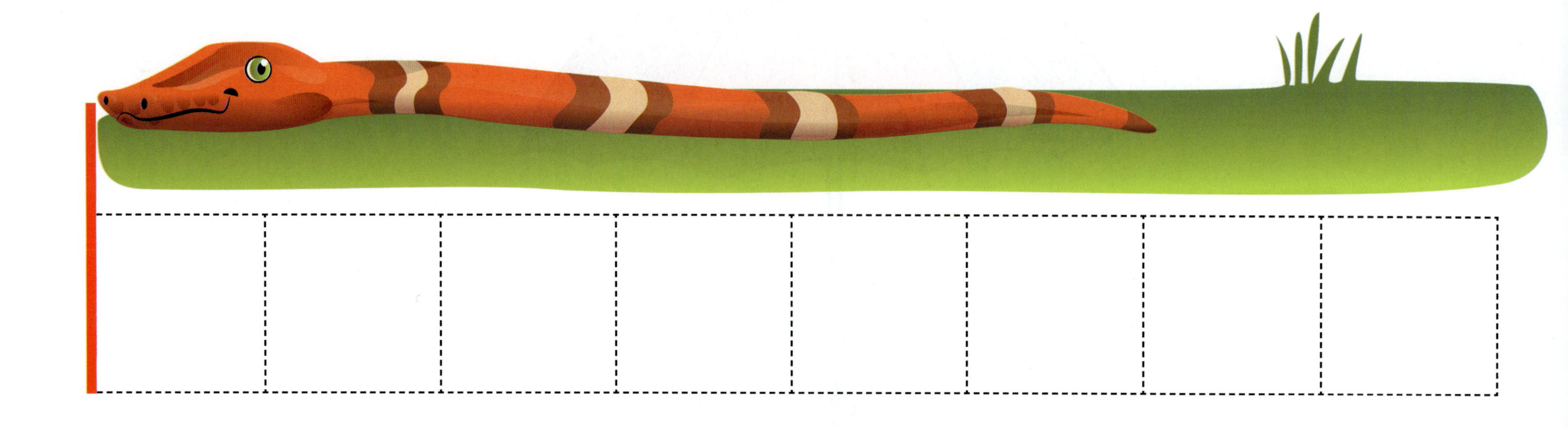

Objectives: Begin to measure using squares.

Listen. Match the objects to the animals.

Match the animals with the food.

Exploration and Knowing of the World

Learning to Do

Think!
What do you like to eat?

Objectives: Associate pets with food.

Listen. What is missing? Draw.

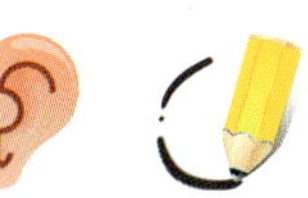

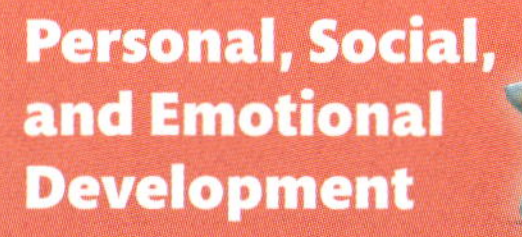

Number the steps to make dog treats.

Think!
What can you do for a pet?

Objectives: Helping others.

Listen Why does Utah think he's smart? 111

Circle what Utah likes to eat.

Objectives: Understand and retell a story.

Draw your favorite word with a /u/ sound. Show a friend and say.

Objectives: Short /u/ sound.

Point, say, and color.

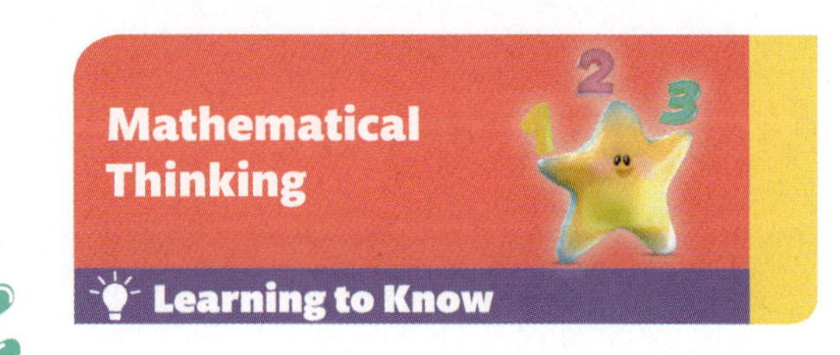

Objectives: Recognize and extend a simple pattern.

Look at the pictures. Trace.

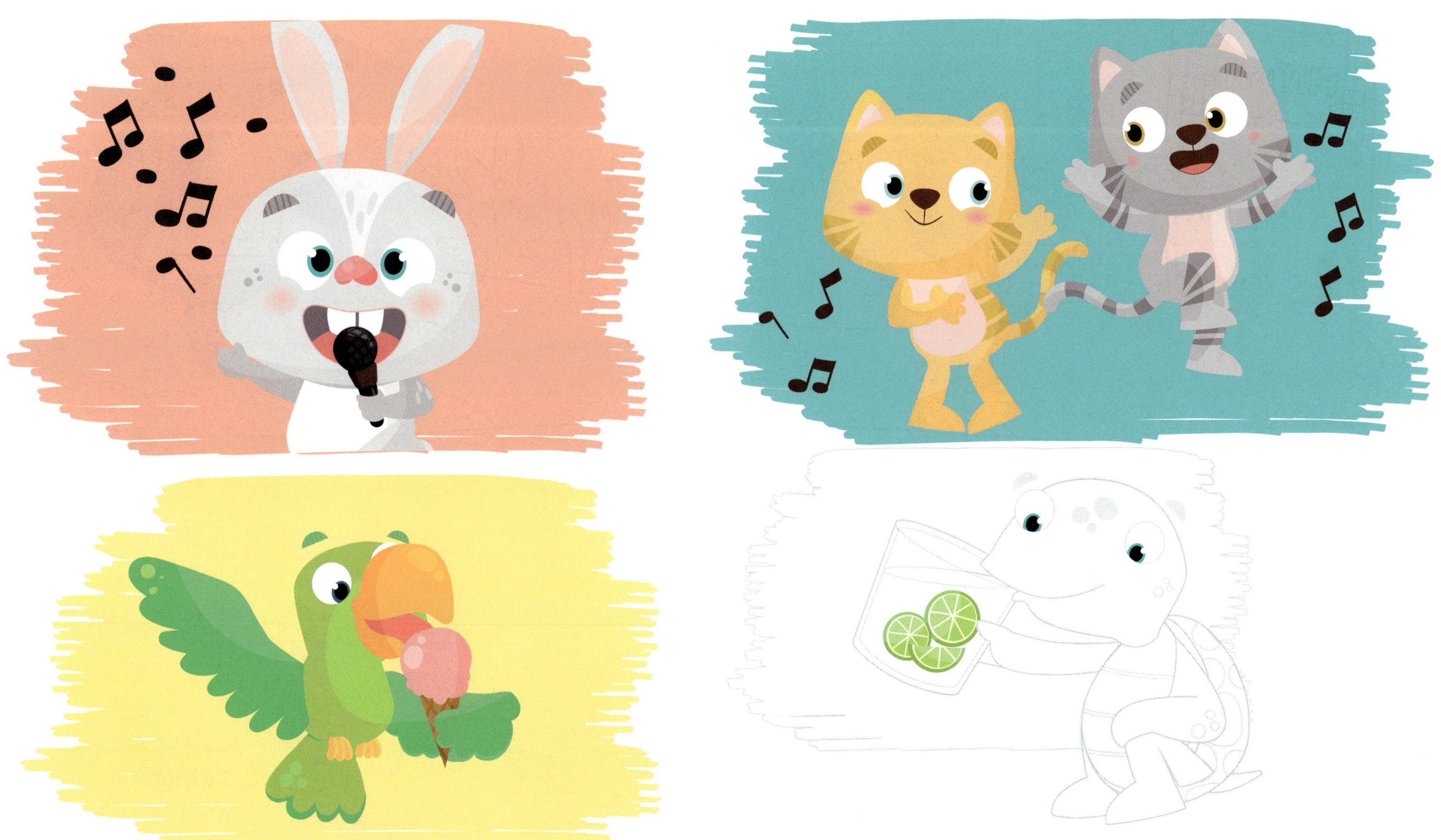

Listen. What are the animals doing?

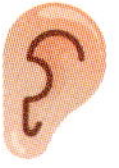

Objectives: Retell a story with body language.

Color the dolphins' and shark's habitat with finger paint.

Exploration and Knowing of the World

Learning to Do

Why do the dolphins win?

Objectives: Talk about different animals.

Look at the picture. What is a vet? What does a vet do?

Circle what a doctor does.

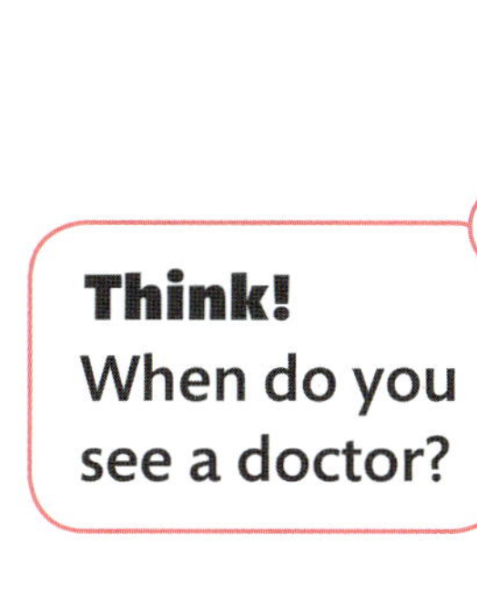

Objectives: Recognize when someone needs help.

What is your favorite food?

Listen to the story. Circle the fruit Uncle Mac wants. Color the *o*'s and *u*.

An Orange for Uncle Mac

What do you like best?

Objectives: Listen to, answer questions, and retell a story.

Match the pictures to the letters. Say.

Objectives: Identify short /o/ and /u/ sounds.

Trace the numbers. Draw and count.

Objectives: Match numbers with objects to 9.

Language Instruction and Communication

Learning to Know

What are they buying at the supermarket?

Draw what you want to buy at the supermaket.

Objectives: Learn food words.

Listen. Circle Charlie Chili's favorite food. 118

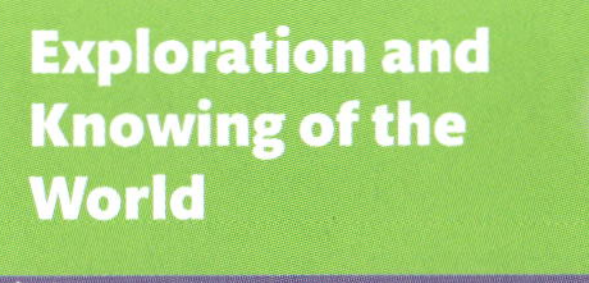

Think!
What food don't you like?

Check the food you like best.

Objectives: Recognize food from different places.

Look at the picture and listen. 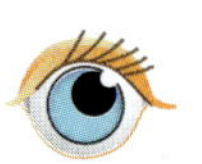 

Personal, Social, and Emotional Development

Learning to Live Together
Learning to Live with Others

What does Jemima need to do? Circle. 

1. 

2. 

3. 

Think!
How do you stay clean?

Objectives: Personal hygiene.

Listen and retell the story.

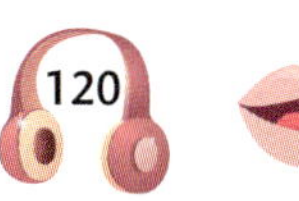

Complete the words.

Hot Dog

Objectives: Listen to, answer questions, and retell a story.

Trace the correct word. Say. 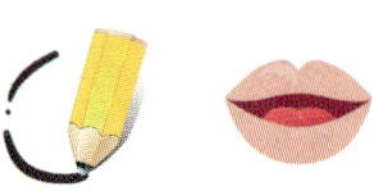

Look up / under.

Draw a BIG orange in the tree. 

Objectives: Short /o/ and /u/ sounds.

Point, say, and trace.

Objectives: Trace numbers 8, 9, and 0.

What color are these fruits? Color.  

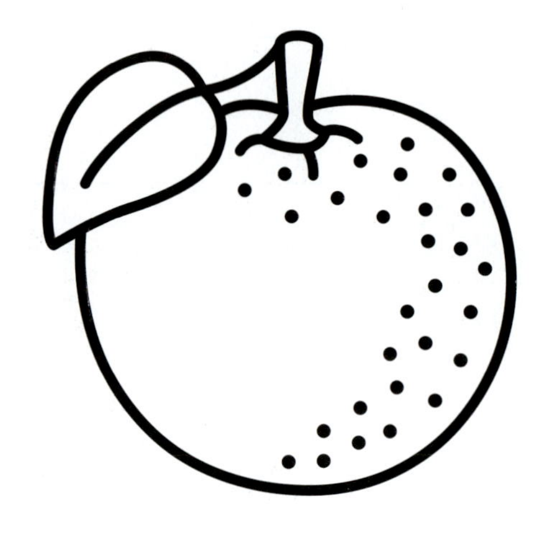

Listen and make the colors. 

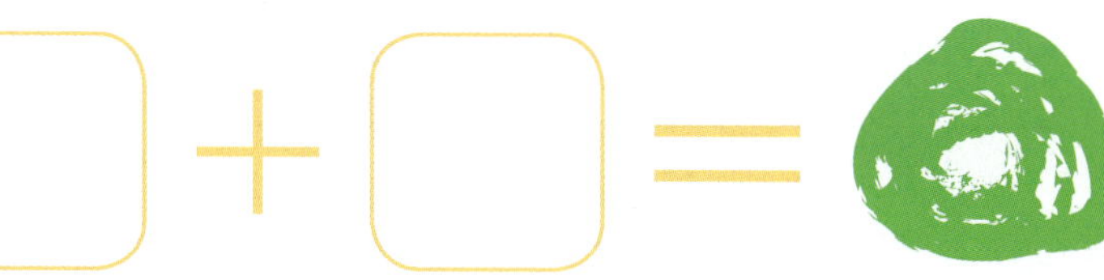

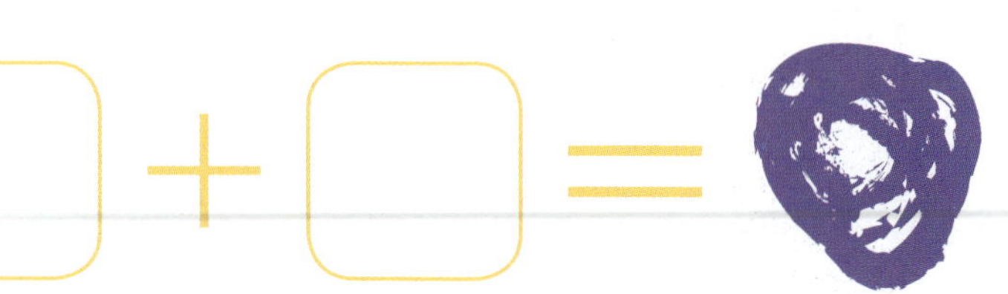

Think!
What fruit is blue?

Objectives: Talk about different colors.

Listen. Circle the food you like best.

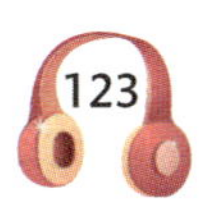

Exploration and Knowing of the World

Learning to Do

What did Hamilton Hamburger almost forget? Draw.

Objectives: Recognize food from different places.

What does Oleg like? What doesn't Oleg like?

Check the things you like. Cross out the things you don't like. ✓ ✗

Think!
What food do you love/hate?

Objectives: Talk about likes and dislikes.

Listen. What's Oswald making? Draw. 124

Who's eating the apple pie?

Objectives: Listen to, answer questions, and retell a story.

Listen. Draw circles on the bug. 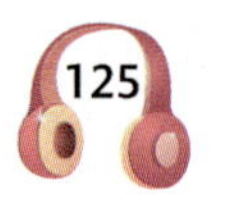  

Draw a triangle around the sound in .

Objectives: Short /o/ and /u/ sound.

Point, say, cut, and paste.

Mathematical Thinking

Learning to Know

Food

Plastic

Paper

Objectives: Sort objects for recycling.

Listen. Circle what Silvia wants. 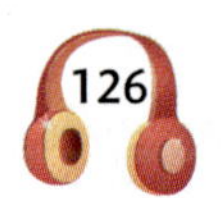 

Check what you want for lunch. Cross out what you don't want for lunch. ✓ X

Objectives: Talk about what they want.

Look at the food. Listen to the doctor.

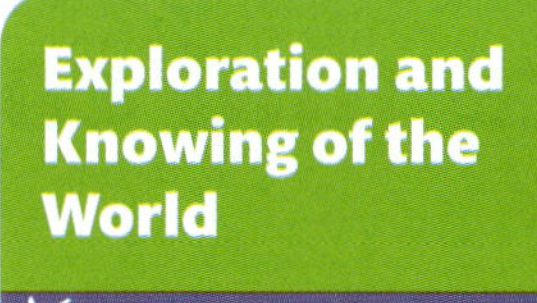

Circle the food that is good for you.

Objectives: Develop awareness of oneself and food.

Trace and color the pictures.  

Personal, Social, and Emotional Development

Learning to Live Together
Learning to Live with Others

Think!
What happens when you eat food that is good for you?

Objectives: Take care of and respect themselves and others.

Listen. Circle where onions grow. 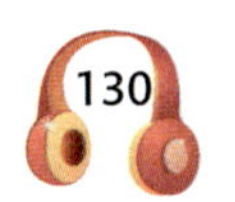 

Draw another vegetable that grows underground.

Objectives: Listen to, answer questions, and retell a story.

Trace the *o*'s in red and the *u*'s in green.

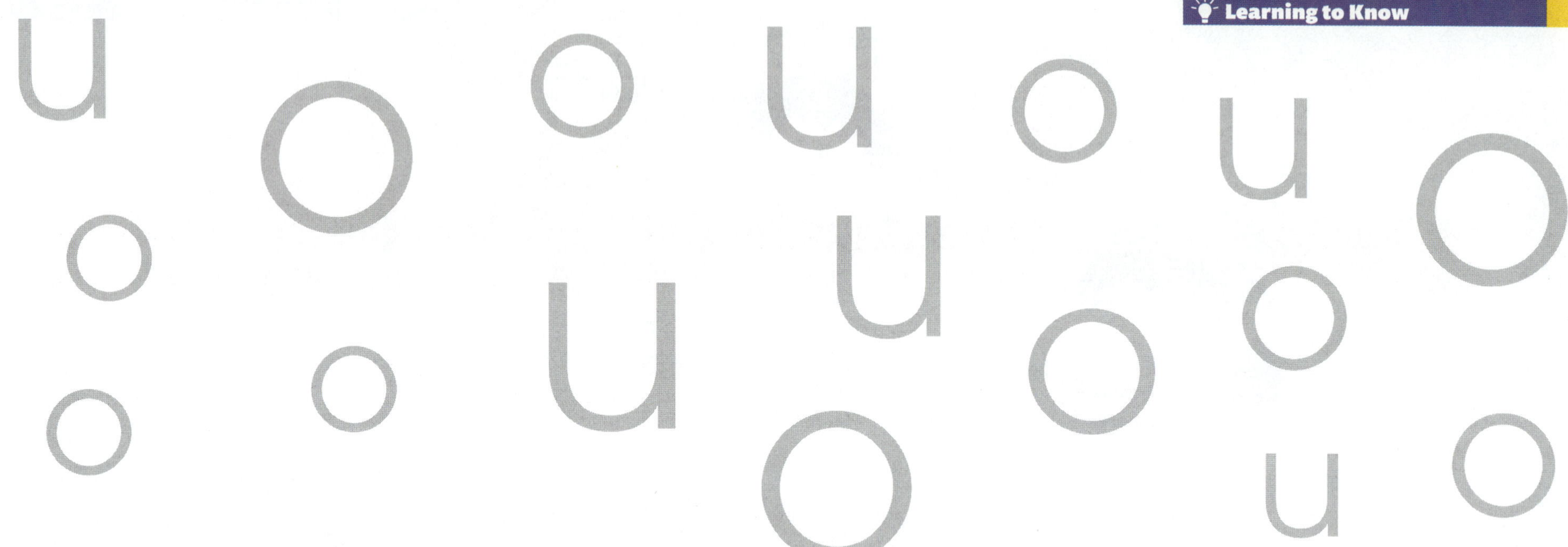

Say the words.

Objectives: Short /o/ and /u/ sounds.

Point. Count the squares.  

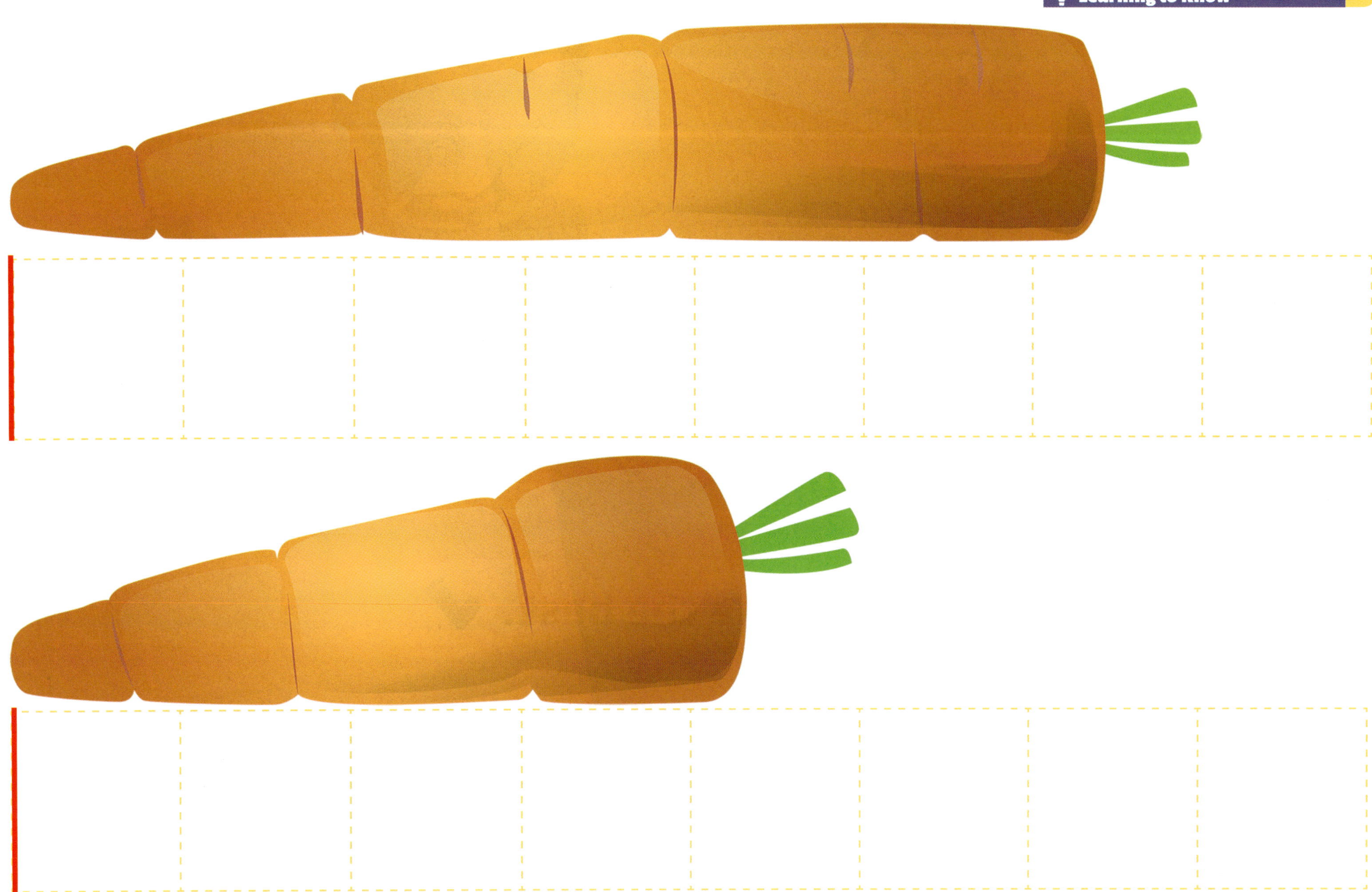

Objectives: Measure using non-standard units.

Listen. Number the steps.

Check the sandwich you like the best.

Objectives: Understand and follow instructions.

Listen. Check Spiky Spaghetti's favorite Italian food. 131

Exploration and Knowing of the World

Learning to Do

What Italian food do you like?

Objectives: Recognize food from different places.

Listen. Circle the food some children don't like.

Personal, Social, and Emotional Development

Learning to Live Together
Learning to Live with Others

Think!
Do you share food with your friends? Why?

Draw food you like for your party.

Objectives: Talk about likes and dislikes.

Unit 8 What do you like about school?

- Listen. Where's the octopus? Draw and color. 136

- Draw Ozzie and Ulaya.

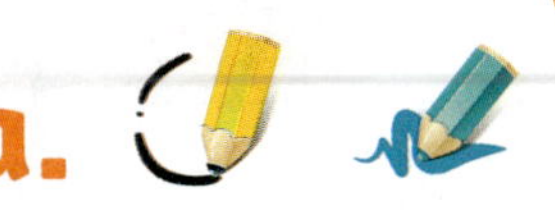

Objectives: Read, answer questions, and retell a story.

Phonemic Awareness

Learning to Know

Listen and circle. 137

o u u u o u u u u u o u u o u o o u u o u o u o u u o o o

ostrich hen puppy

What animals do you hear?

Objectives: Short /o/ and /u/ sounds.

Count and say. Trace. Write.

0 1 2 3 4 5 6 7 8 9 10

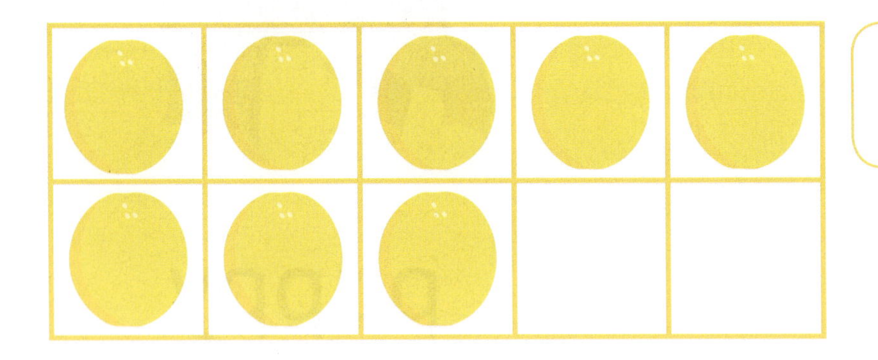

Objectives: Identify numbers 5 to 10.

What's the teacher saying?

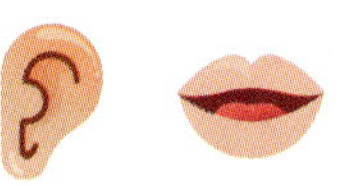

Listen. Draw the picture. Say the word.

Objectives: Understand and follow instructions and rules.

What can he do? What can she do?

Listen. What else can they do?

Think!
Can boys and girls do the same things?

Objectives: Recognize that boys and girls can do the same activities.

Get the tiddlywinks in the cup. Play and say.

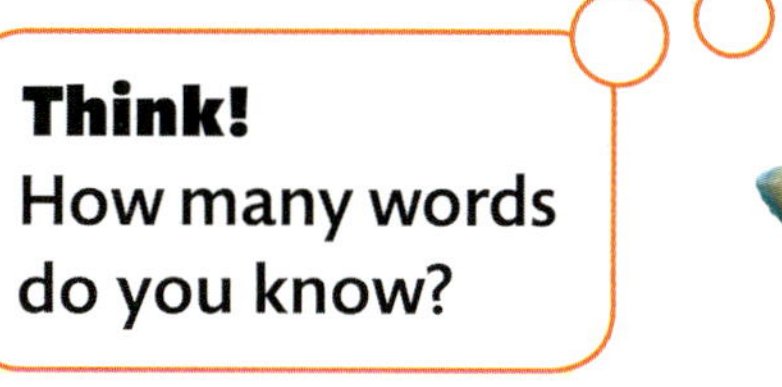

Objectives: Play games following rules.

Listen. Circle the *o* and *u*. Write your name with cutouts.

Objectives: Read, answer questions, and retell a story.

- **Paste pieces of paper to form the letters.**

- **Tell a friend an *o* word and a *u* word.** 

Objectives: Short /o/ and /u/ sounds.

Point and say. Trace. 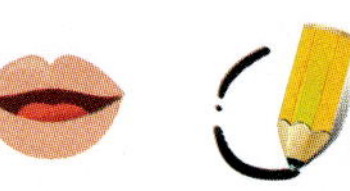

0 0 0 0

1 1 1 1

2 2 2 2

3 3 3 3

4 4 4 4

5 5 5 5

6 6 6 6

7 7 7 7

8 8 8 8

9 9 9 9

Objectives: Trace all digits from 0 to 9.

What can the children do? Check the things you can do.

What else can you do?

Objectives: Abilities.

- **Talk about the shapes in the puzzle. Circle the square.**

- **Trace the triangles to make a square. Color.**

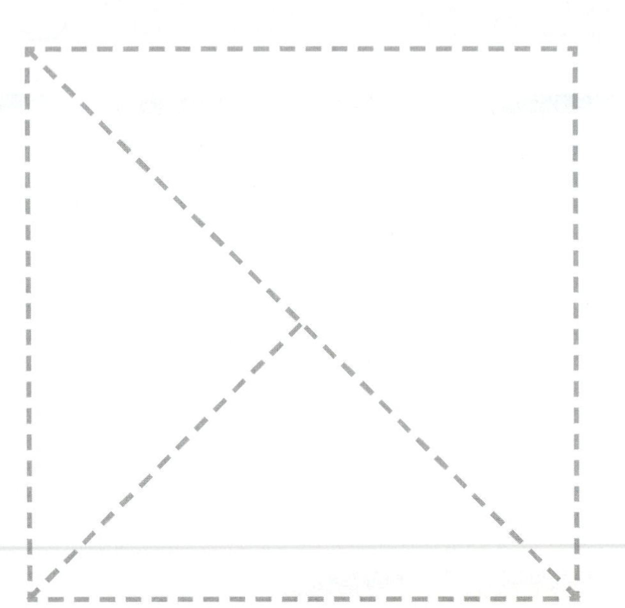

Objectives: Associate objects, shapes, and colors.

Listen. Find Peter, Sammy, Meg, and Alison.

Think!
How are you the same as other children? Different?

Draw yourself in the sandpit.

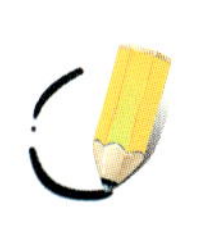

Objectives: Describe themselves.

Listen. Circle the title of the story. 142

Draw your favorite character.

Objectives: Read, answer questions, and retell a story.

- **Draw a picture with *o* and *u* words. Tell a friend about your picture.**

Objectives: Short /o/ and /u/ sounds.

Point. Count the squares.

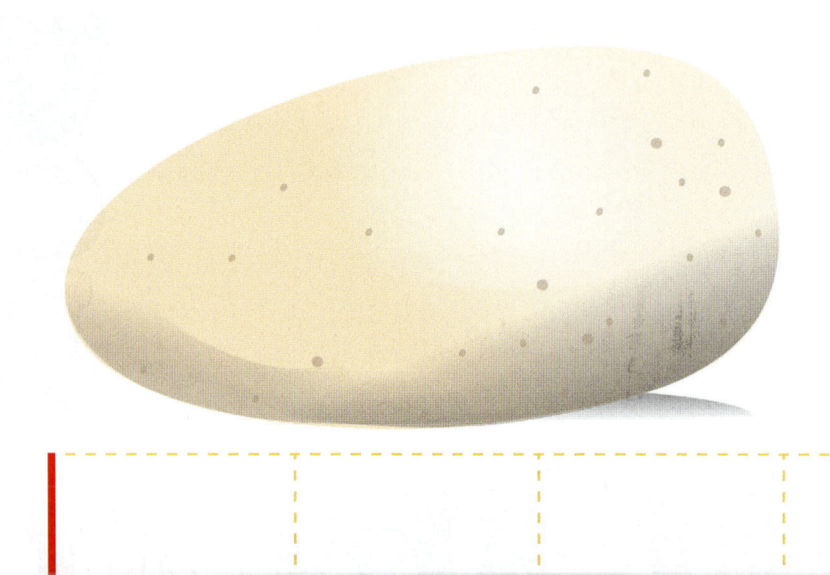

Objectives: Measure using non-standard units.

Listen. Where are the things?

Listen. Put the objects in the right place.

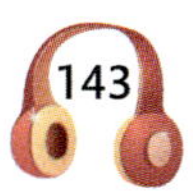

Objectives: Talk about location of objects.

What are Jack and Jill doing?

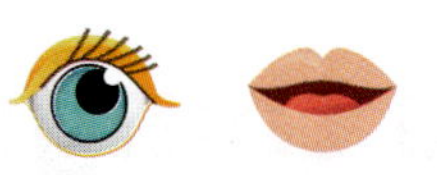

Number the steps.

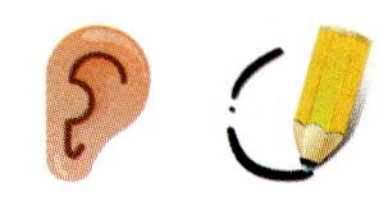

Objectives: Recognize that boys and girls can do the same activities.

Are the children being nice to each other? Color.

Think!
How can you be nice to someone today?

Objectives: Respect others.

Listen and answer some questions.

Who rescues the hula hoop? Circle.

Objectives: Read, answer questions, and retell a story.

Listen and circle.  

Think and draw.

Mathematical Thinking

Learning to Know

Objectives: Identify favorite math activities.

What can you see? Act out the conversation.

Where are the crayons? Draw.

Objectives: Understand and follow instructions.

Find out about Tamagotchi pets.

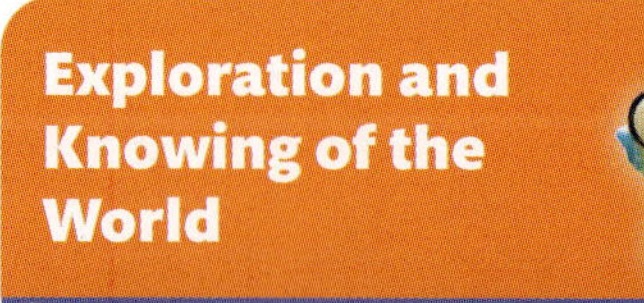

Check the electronic toys you have.

Objectives: Compare personal knowledge with what they hear.

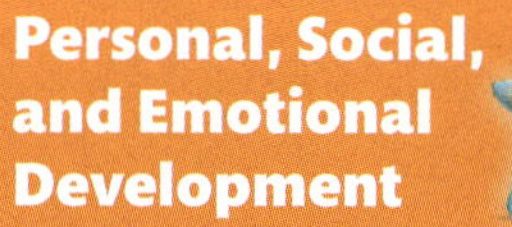

Match the toys to the children.

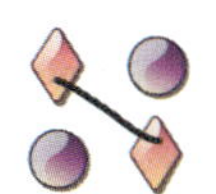

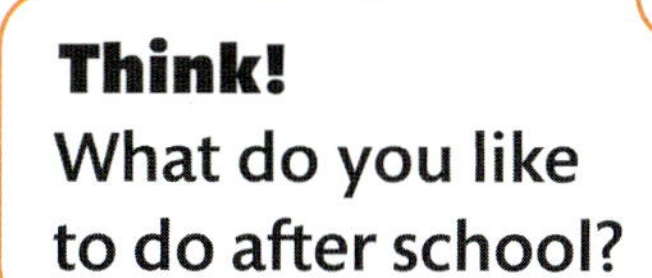

Draw yourself with your favorite toy.

Objectives: Talk about likes and dislikes.

Unit 2, page 50

Unit 1, page 25

Unit 5, page 131

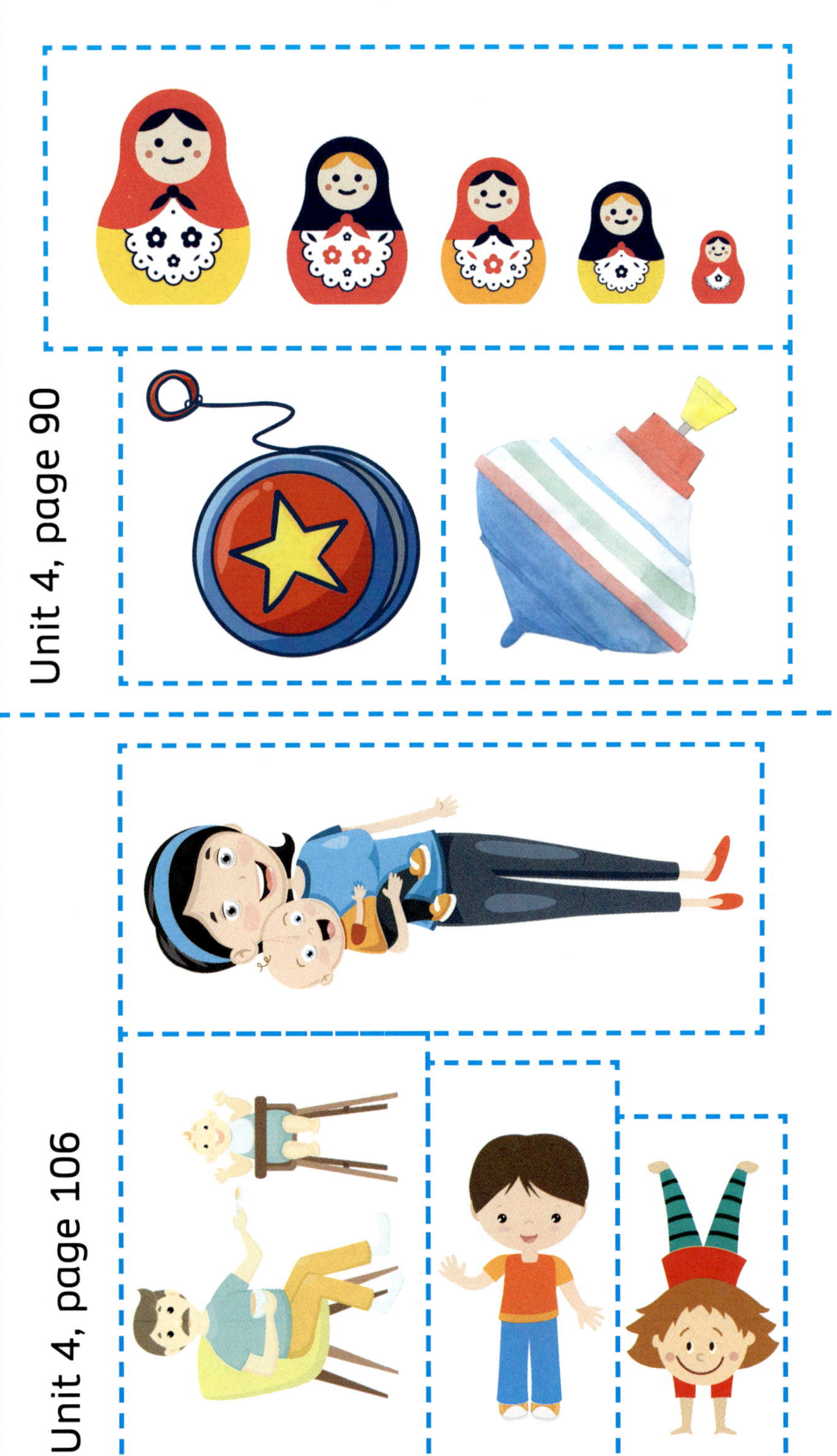

Unit 6, page 156

Mathematical Thinking, Pattern Blocks

Mathematical Thinking, Pattern Blocks

Mathematical Thinking, Pattern Blocks

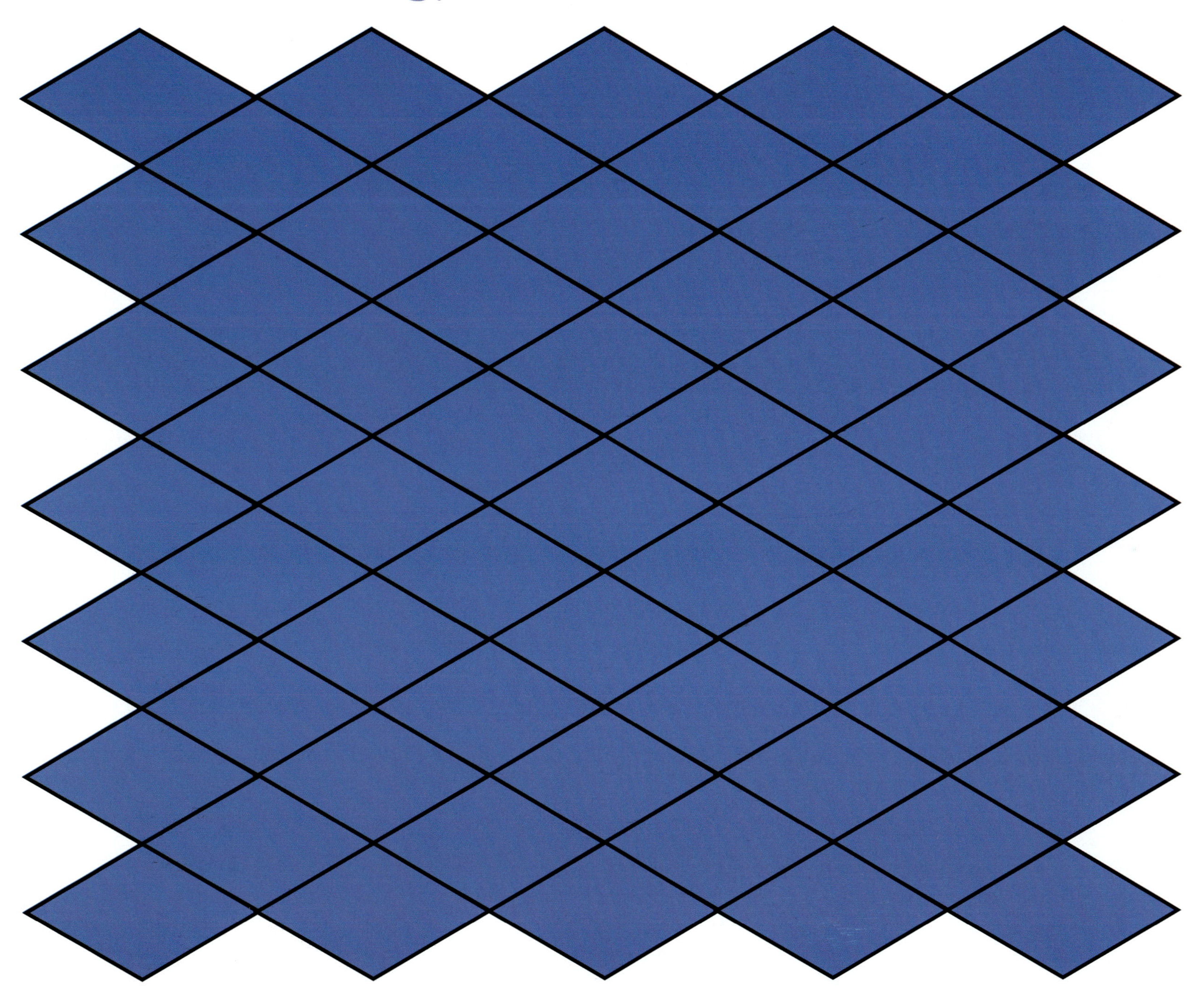

Mathematical Thinking, Pattern Blocks

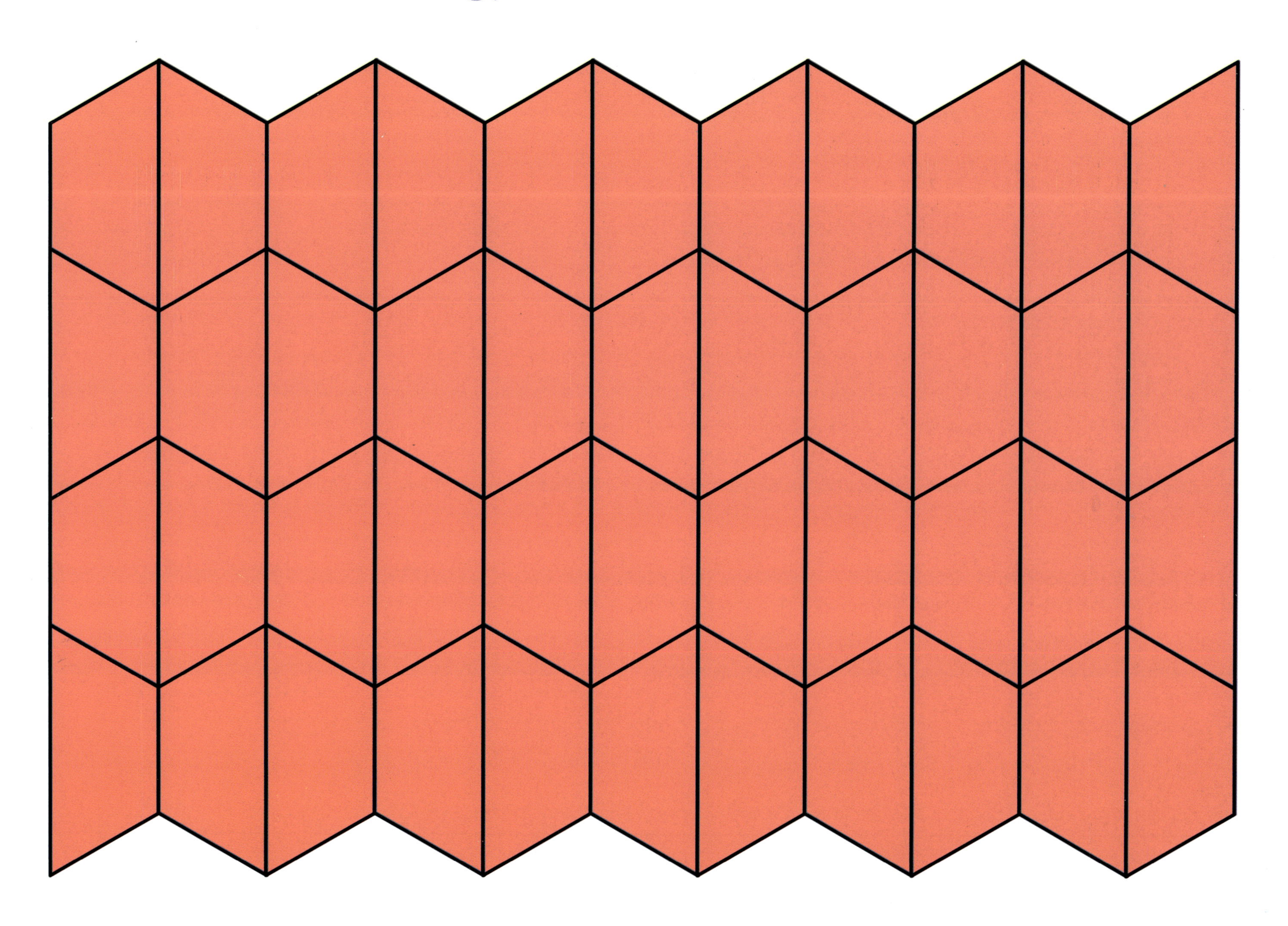

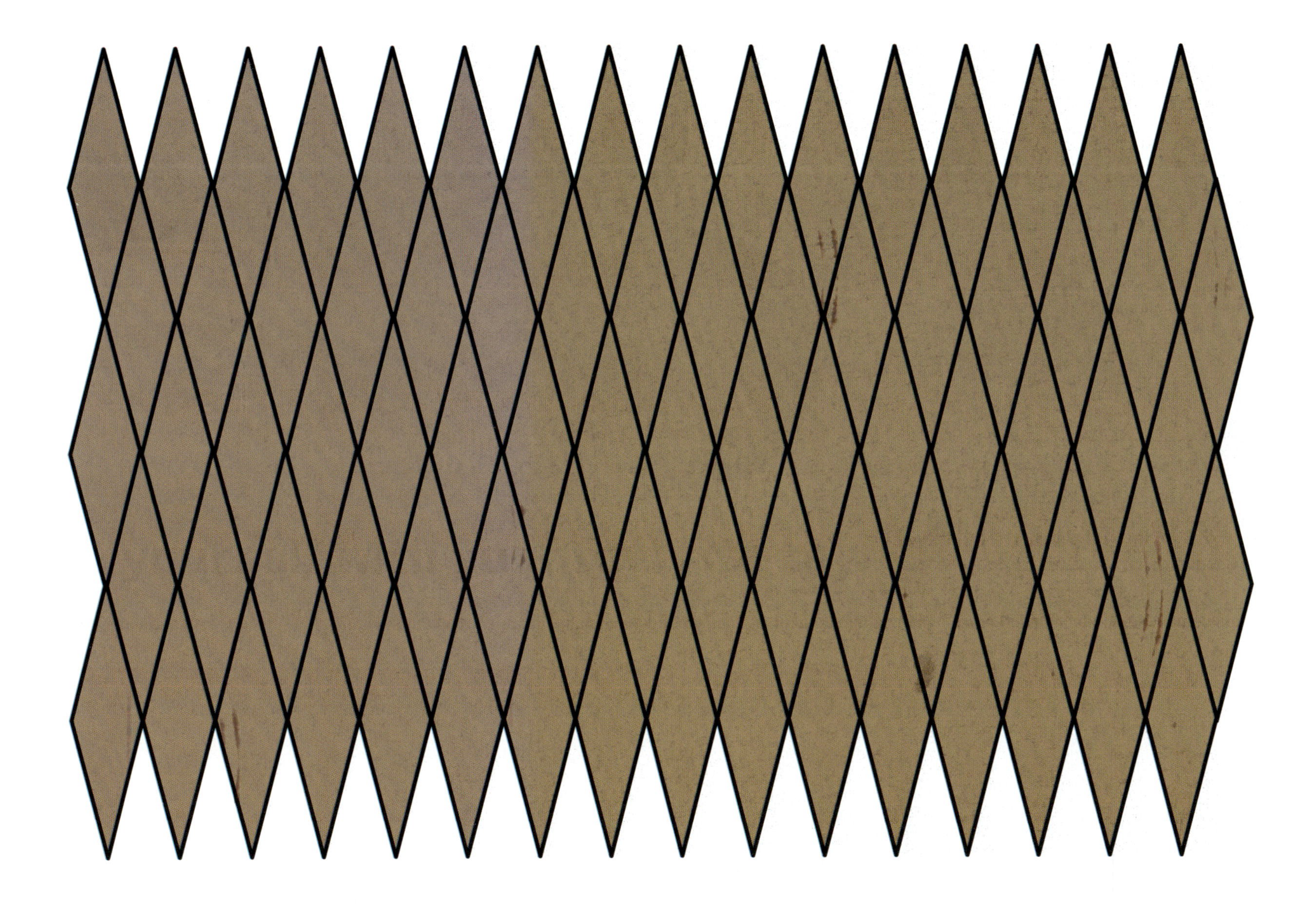

Mathematical Thinking, Pattern Blocks

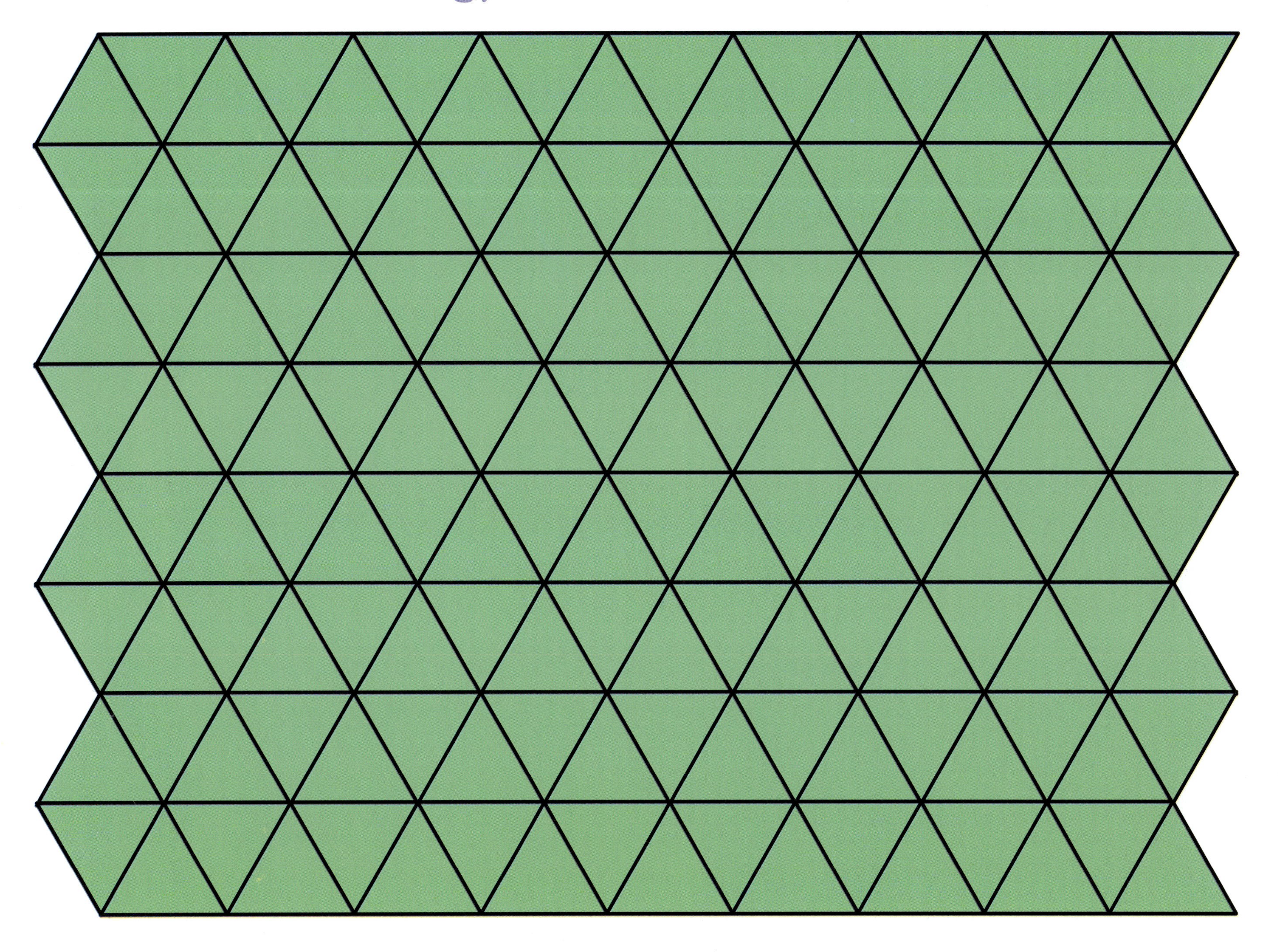

My Starfish 50 Chart

1	2	3	4	5	6	7	8	9	10
11	12	13	14	15	16	17	18	19	20
21	22	23	24	25	26	27	28	29	30
31	32	33	34	35	36	37	38	39	40
41	42	43	44	45	46	47	48	49	50